CALM BEFORE THE FIRE-STORM

On July 15, a strange and eerie hush settled over Germany. The silence—the absence of the massed motors droning deeply in the sky—was almost a crash of soundlessness. For several days and nights the skies remained clear, and soon the Germans in cities all across the Reich turned to look wonderingly at one another.

This respite from attack—it was wonderful and it gave one a chance to breathe deeply and to relax. But it was wrong, for the bombers were still there.

For ten days and ten nights Germany suffered no attacks. By the tenth day the tension was almost unbearable. It was a frightening suspense.

And with good reason. *Gomorrah* was about to be unleashed.

THE BANTAM WAR BOOK SERIES

This series of books is about a world on fire.

The carefully chosen volumes in the Bantam War Book Series cover the full dramatic sweep of World War II. Many are eyewitness accounts by the men who fought in a global conflict as the world's future hung in the balance. Fighter pilots, tank commanders and infantry captains, among many others, recount exploits of individual courage. They present vivid portraits of brave men, true stories of gallantry, moving sagas of survival and stark tragedies of untimely death.

In 1933 Nazi Germany marched to become an empire that was to last a thousand years. In only twelve years that empire was destroyed, and ever since, the country has been bisected by her conquerors. Italy relinquished her colonial lands, as did Japan. These were the losers. The winners also lost the empires they had so painfully seized over the centuries. And one, Russia, lost over twenty million dead.

Those wartime 1940s were a simple, even a hopeful time. Hats came in only two colors, white and black, and after an initial battering the Allied nations started on a long and laborious march toward victory. It was a time when sane men believed the world would evolve into a decent place, but, as with all futures, there was no one then who could really forecast the world that we know now.

There are many ways to think about war. It has always been hard to understand the motivations and braveries of Axis soldiers fighting to enslave and dominate their neighbors. Yet it is impossible to know the hammer without the anvil, and to comprehend ourselves we must know the people we once fought against.

Through these books we can discover what it was like to take part in the war that was a final experience for nearly fifty million human beings. In so doing we may discover the strength to make a world as good as the one contained in those dreams and aspirations once believed by heroic men. We must understand our past as an honor to those dead who can no longer choose. They exchanged their lives in a hope for this future that we now inhabit. Though the fight took place many years ago, each of us remains as a living part of it.

THE NIGHT HAMBURG DIED

MARTIN CAIDIN

BANTAM BOOKS
NEW YORK · TORONTO · LONDON · SYDNEY · AUCKLAND

This book is for George E. Haddaway, a
close friend and mentor for many years,
who has never yet allowed me to finish
a sentence.

*This edition contains the complete text
of the original hardcover edition.
NOT ONE WORD HAS BEEN OMITTED.*

THE NIGHT HAMBURG DIED

*A Bantam Book / published by arrangement with
the author*

PRINTING HISTORY

Bantam edition / November 1990

ISBN 0-553-28784-2

Published simultaneously in the United States and Canada

*Bantam Books are published by Bantam Books, a division of
Bantam Doubleday Dell Publishing Group, Inc. Its trademark,
consisting of the words "Bantam Books" and the portrayal of a
rooster, is Registered in U.S. Patent and Trademark Office and in
other countries. Marca Registrada. Bantam Books, 666 Fifth
Avenue, New York, New York 10103.*

PRINTED IN THE UNITED STATES OF AMERICA

OPM   0 9 8 7 6 5 4 3 2 1

CONTENTS

NORTH SEA

FRISIAN ISLANDS

ZUIDER ZEE

Amsterdam

HOLLAND

Essen

Ruhr R.

Mülheim

Remsheid

Krefeld

WESTPHALIA

Brussels

Cologne

BELGIUM

PAS DE CALAIS

Aachen

ARDENNES

LUXEMBOURG

FRANCE

GERMANY AND
THE LOWLANDS

Scale of Miles

0 10 20 30 40 50 60 70 80 90

FOREWORD

Nearly fifty years ago the Battle of Britain entered its phase of mass incendiary raids as, night after night, German bombers smashed at the heart of London. For long months in daylight the Germans had fought to break the back of the English in the heaviest aerial attacks ever known in warfare. The skill and determination of a handful of young British fighter pilots in their agile Spitfires and Hurricanes doomed that attempt to failure.

Hurricane

What the Germans could not do under the sun, they struggled to achieve beneath the stars. Their Dorniers and Heinkels and Junkers came over in heavier and heavier night raids, gutting large sections of the English capital with an avalanche of incendiary bombs.

One of the spectators during the height of this nocturnal blitz was a man whom the Germans would soon come to know with a fierce and bitter hatred. He was Sir Arthur Harris, the Marshal of the Royal Air Force. The bombers he commanded in those grim days represented only a token striking force. They were slow and unwieldy and terribly vulnerable to the enemy's swift fighters. The hope of returning to German cities the fiery devastation blazing in London was dim indeed; it lay in fact beyond even the speculation of the weary British who suffered the flames of German aerial attack.

Sir Arthur Harris looked out upon a forbidding sight. An ocean of fire heaved and swelled in the heart of London. He could see the lofty dome of St. Paul's standing out in stark contrast against the fierce flames beyond. That night, as he felt the heat of the flames and listened to the crashing din of exploding bombs and antiaircraft guns, Harris turned to a fellow officer and remarked quietly: "Well, they are sowing the wind."

It was a simple statement, almost a hopeless one, considering the circumstances; yet it was uttered with the absolute conviction that the Germans were indeed sowing the wind of an unbelievable storm of destruction from the bombers that he—Harris—would before too long order far into German skies. It was one of the most prophetic remarks of all military history.

Less than two years later Harris's prophecy bore its savage fruit. During the ten days of July 24 to August 3 of 1943, heavy Lancaster and Halifax bombers commanded by Sir Arthur Harris accomplished the most gruesome task of aerial bombardment ever known to man. In a sea of flames hurled upon the proud German city of Hamburg, they achieved a height of destruction and terror beyond all human experience. The bombers struck again and again in massive blows from the dark German skies, compounding terror into a horror that defies all description.

Hamburg was a city of nearly two million people; it was one of the world's finest ports and an outstanding industrial center. Because of its vital position in the German war economy, Hamburg stood high on the list of cities to be "obliterated." The British almost literally achieved this terrible goal.

Gomorrah was the code name assigned to the effort of the Bomber Command of the Royal Air Force to "take out" the city of Hamburg. In their ten days of sustained attack they released an incredible avalanche of steel and explosives and fire into the thriving port.

Hamburg that week was trampled beneath the colossal tread of storms of fire unprecedented in all history. A unique combination of the bombs, the weather, and the high density of buildings produced a phenomenon known as the *firestorm*, a fiery giant that reared thousands of feet over the terror-striken city and lashed Hamburg mercilessly. Tens of thousands of people died in an agony of sustained fire never known before, or since. Not even Hiroshima and Nagasaki, suffering the smashing blows of nuclear explosions, could match the utter hell of Hamburg.

In the bombing of Britain, the heaviest blow by the German Air Force was unquestionably the gutting of the city of Coventry. In a raid lasting many hours German bombers did their utmost to wipe Coventry from the face of the earth. When the explosions ceased and the flames died out from want of fuel, more than a hundred acres of the British city had vanished, leaving only ruins and ashes.

One hundred acres, and Coventry stood as a memorial of devastation.

In those terrible ten days of mid-1943, the British bombers gutted *more than six thousand acres of Hamburg.*

"For weeks afterward," states an official German document, "eyewitnesses were unable to report without succumbing to their nerves and weeping hysterically. They would try to speak, then would break down and cry: 'I can't stand seeing it again; I can't stand it!'"

A woman who survived Hamburg was interviewed weeks later; she still had not recovered from the shock of her experiences in the flaming, shattered city: "I saw people killed by falling bricks and heard the screams of others dying in the fire. I dragged my best friend from a burning building and she died in my arms. *I saw others who went stark mad.* The shock to my nerves and to the soul, one can never erase."

The Police President of Hamburg reported of his smashed city that: "Its horror is revealed in the howling and raging of the firestorms, the hellish noise of exploding bombs and the death cries of martyred human beings as well as in the big silence after the raids. Speech is impotent to portray the measure of the horror, which shook the people for ten days and nights and the traces of which were written indelibly on the face of the city and its inhabitants. . . .

"No flight of imagination will ever succeed in measuring and describing the gruesome scenes of horror in the many buried air raid shelters. Posterity can only bow its head in honor of the fate of these innocents, sacrificed by the murderous lust of a sadistic enemy. . . ."

Such is an excerpt from an official German document, eloquent in its description of horror. Yet it is difficult indeed for many survivors of Nazi terror to accept at face value the German outcry that "innocents were sacrificed by the murderous lust of a sadistic enemy . . ." Dachau and Belsen have tarnished the claims of the "innocents," but then this book does not attempt to measure the inevitable slaughter of German civilians in mass air raids against the subhuman depravity of deliberate and calculated genocide in gas ovens and experimental chambers.

Hamburg is a chapter of war unmatched by any other incident known to man. More people have died in other aerial attacks than succumbed in the flaming ten days that seared Hamburg. At Hiroshima an estimated eighty thousand people perished in the explosion of the atomic bomb and the firestorm that raged for hours afterward. A sweep conflagration in Tokyo the night of March 9, 1945, took the lives of at least 84,000 human beings within a few hours, although postwar Japanese statements claim that 130,000 people perished that night.

But none of these can compare to Hamburg, where the fire and horror lasted ten full days. This is what makes Hamburg—and the loss of some seventy thousand men, women, and children—stand out as the worst of the disasters visited upon civilization during the insanity of World War II.

It is difficult, perhaps impossible, for one reading this story nearly fifty years after the fact, to understand fully what took place in Hamburg in the summer of 1943. But the reader may gain some realization of the scope of destruction if he considers Boston, and the forty-odd communities—cities and towns—that constitute the Boston metropolitan area.

In size, industry, and port facilities this is roughly the kind of urban target which the British planners saw before them. The two cities separated by thousands of miles were strangely comparable in population as well.

Consider Boston, then—a city with which we can familiarize ourselves so much better. Consider an attack lasting ten days and nights—interludes of freedom from attack culminating in intense bombardment and resurgence of the towering flames. Imagine more than fifty per cent of metropolitan Boston smashed into ruin and filled with decaying bodies. Take every single building in the corporate limits of Boston proper, and pound it to wreckage, burn everything that can be consumed by fire, kill tens of thousands of people. Imagine Boston destroyed in this manner, left in ruins and ash and pestilential stench.

Imagine all this in its worst—and you understand Hamburg in its reality.

When the bombers had finished, a wave of utter terror radiated from the stricken city, sensed in other cities as the first fingers of panic; later, this panic would explode in wild fury as the rain of bombs continued, moving across Germany to concentrate on new targets. There was another kind of fear as well.

"We were of the opinion," stated Albert Speer, the Reichsminister for Armaments, "that a rapid repetition of this type of attack upon another six German towns would inevitably cripple the will to sustain armament manufacture and war production. It was I who first verbally reported to the Fuehrer at that time that a continuation of these attacks might bring about a rapid end to the war."

This book is the story of that devastating attack, which ended only because Hamburg had ceased to exist as a city. It lay blackened, desolate, and gutted; fear prowled the ruins where not even a single rat had survived the flames.

Over the last nine years I have spoken to many Germans who survived Hamburg, and to many British pilots and crew members who sowed the fire through the city. Even today they are fully clear in their reports; time has failed to dim the clarity of so stupendous an emotional experience.

Hamburg was destroyed more than two years before the atomic bomb was first exploded as a weapon against a city.

But even the debacle of Hamburg will be as nothing against the holocaust of thermonuclear bombs. For the sake of mankind's future existence, have we heeded the lesson?

MARTIN CAIDIN

New York, 1960
(updated 1990)

1

THE TARGET

Hamburg was the second largest city in the Reich, its prewar population of 1,760,000 swollen to two million by the influx of workers for the shipyards, docks, and other industries. It was the busiest port on the continent of Europe, and it was also the largest producing center of U-boats in all Germany.

Within the environs of this major industrial center were more than three thousand industrial establishments, and more than five thousand commercial firms, almost all of them engaged in the vital transport and shipping industries for which Hamburg was famous.

Every one of the major shipyards and the majority of the lesser yards were working day and night on the construction of submarines. This one city alone built more than forty-five per cent of all German undersea raiders. Here was located the most renowned works of all such industrial complexes, the famed Blohm and Voss Shipyards—the same company which had gained international repute for its giant seaplanes and flying boats in prewar times. Of equal importance in Hamburg were the Europaische

Tanklager and Transport A.G., the Rhenania Ossag distillation plant, and Ernst Schliemann's works at Wilhelmsburg.

In Hamburg also were the Deutsche Petroleum A.G. refineries, Theodor Zeise at Altona (the second largest manufacturer of ships' screws), and the largest wool combing plant of the Hamburger Wollkammerai A.G.

The wharves of Hamburg were busy through the daylight and under the hours of darkness. Despite its size, the armaments industry burst its seams steadily in an unending expansion program. There were industries for the production of food, and other industries that manufactured all sorts of industrial machinery, electrical and precision instruments, chemicals, and components of military aircraft.

As an entrepôt center (*Umschlaghafen*) for shipping and trading with European countries, and as a vital supply base for German troops in Northern and Western Europe, the thriving port of Hamburg was a well-oiled cog in the German war machine. And from the port itself, canals radiated out like capillaries in a fanlike projection, crowded at all times with barges carrying munitions, fuel supplies, and raw materials for the city's industry.

Rich in tradition and history, the ancient Hanseatic town of Hamburg enjoyed all the advantages of a superb geographical location on the Elbe, seventy-five miles from the river mouth at Cuxhaven. Even in the years preceding World War II Hamburg flourished as the Continent's largest and busiest seaport.

Hamburg proper straddles both sides of the little

River Alster which, dammed up a short distance from its mouth, gives the city the pleasure of a lake created just where it was most wanted. The southern portion of this body of water, lying within the line of former military fortifications, is known as the Inner Alster, and the other and larger area, as the Outer Alster. The city's oldest section, which traces its history back for several hundreds of years, extends to the east of the Alster.

To the west is Neustadt, the "new town" which entered the incorporated city in 1678. Just beyond Neustadt lies St. Pauli, a relative newcomer that came into the Hamburg environs in 1876. In the northeast is the ancient community of St. Georg which, although a lively center as far back as the thirteenth century, did not become part of the Hamburg community proper until 1868. As the years passed additional communities entered the expanding metropolis. On April 1, 1938, Hamburg leaped its bounds when the former Prussian towns of Altona, Harburg, and Wandsbek all united with Hamburg. To its citizens the area of 288 square miles that now contained the entire city became known as Gross-Hamburg. This was the city marked for destruction in 1943, a vital wartime shipping and industrial area where lived and worked more than two million people.

Hamburg as a target was peculiarly vulnerable to incendiary attack. The construction of Hamburg followed the pattern established within most of the older German cities. The central portions featured a building density—the ratio of roof area to ground area—of some thirty to forty per cent. This figure is extremely important, for a city with so high a building density is acutely vulnerable to the horrifying holocaust known as the *firestorm*.

The effect of incendiary bomb attack, whether carried out as part of a mass "saturation" raid or as a "precision" attack, is largely a matter of wind conditions. The most excellent bomber formation that lays down a careful pattern may still produce slight results because of the strong and variable wind currents between the bombers and the ground. Providing the city is large enough and the bomber formation properly aligned and concentrated, the deleterious effects of the wind can be overcome. When all the conditions are propitious, however— building density, wind conditions, bomb pattern, concentrated time of attack—then the bombing mission may produce results beyond all expectations.

In Hamburg, the ground conditions were nearly perfect. The *absence* of high ground winds during the peaks of the repeated British assaults meant that the dispersal of the millions of incendiary bombs remained within a close pattern. Splashing into an area with so high a building density, these bombs were almost certain to cause tens of thousands of individual fires within minutes of the attack.

At the core of the city lay the old medieval town, a district offering maximum opportunity to incendiary attack. The buildings were squeezed closely together within narrow and winding streets, and the building density reached an unbelievable fifty to sixty per cent. These structures ranged from three to five stories in height, and averaged about 1,500 square feet in area. They had several tiers of attics, strongly framed in timber, with roof ridges at right angles to the streets.

If the reader has ever walked through the densest section of Boston, or Manhattan's Greenwich Village, he knows the conditions prevailing in Hamburg on the eve of the Royal Air Force onslaught. Not even the ghettos of Harlem with their six-story firetraps could match the inflammability and vulnerability of Hamburg.

Around the "old town" were extensive districts built up in the 18th century. These areas were laid out in a rectangular street pattern, as is common in American cities, and the buildings extended from three to six stories in height. There were on the average larger than the "old town" structures, but rarely exceeded three thousand square feet. Most of these buildings had masonry walls and tile or slate roofs, mounted on wooden battens. Most characteristic within the structures were heavy wooden pugged floors. The latter had a layer of cinders or other inert material between the ceiling and the wooden floor finish above.

Often found in the center of these blocks—the rectangle of the buildings—were the so-called backyard industrial structures of the cities. Even more than the tenement buildings, these were naked to incendiary attack. Their walls were for the most part thin, and they usually contained stores of inflammable fuel.

On the outer ridges (except for the ancient cities that were incorporated into Gross-Hamburg) were the more modern wide streets, here the houses were small, wood floors were common, and the roof-supporting members were of wood—all prime for fire.

The commercial and industrial areas of the cities like Hamburg follow a similar pattern. As the town grows the older residential sections fall in real estate values, and many of them are converted into shops. Soon the vacant spaces between buildings vanish, replaced by small industrial or commercial factories. In the back yards, the space is filled with storage buildings. In this process the deterioration of the older buildings is not the only fire risk. As more of the ground area is filled, the increased building density aggravates even further the danger of massed fires and of fire spread. Finally, the greater amounts of highly combustible materials—kerosene and oil, for instance—favor the rapid growth of fires beyond all control. In anything more than a slight breeze, fire can sweep through such districts with frightening speed.

Up to the evening of July 24, 1943, when, unknown to the Germans, *Gomorrah* was ushered into being by the British, Hamburg had already suffered a total of 137 attacks from the air. The raids extended from nuisance attacks to keep the population jittery, to "heavy bombings"; heavy, at least, on the basis of pre-*Gomorrah* standards.

The British learned from experience early in the war that fire was far more dangerous and effective in destroying buildings and factories than high-explosive bombs. From the results of the German attacks the

Royal Air Force Bomber Command formulated its own offensive policy. High explosive bombs were used on targets susceptible to extensive blast damage, for the piercing of buildings, the wrecking of concrete and steel structures. It was obvious—a natural outgrowth of having suffered similar attack—that the most effective raid was one that used both the high explosive bomb and a mass shower of incendiaries.

The British pattern utilized the greatest strength of both weapons, pouring a mixture of explosive and incendiary missiles into the city. The explosive missiles smashed water-main networks and shattered communications, making concerted fire fighting difficult. Craters and collapsed buildings blocked roads and streets, often making them impassable. The bombs tore open buildings, smashed windows, and ripped roofing free—exposing the highly combustible materials within to the direct effects of incendiaries as well as facilitating the spread of fires started by the incendiary bombs.

But a raid of mixed explosive and incendiary bombs serves still another purpose. Even a mass attack of incendiary bombs can usually be dealt with by a skilled fire fighting and civil defense organization. Many of the bombs can be extinguished, or rendered harmless, before the flames can spread seriously. The British knew from their own experiences that their fire guard had saved vast sections of British cities, and they did not doubt that the Germans were equally well trained and heroic.

Since the most effective defense against the incendiary bomb was the fire service, the men and women of this service automatically become a prime target. The incendiaries would cause more than eighty to ninety per cent of all the fires in the city—if the fire services could be kept out of action. And that is where the explosive bombs did their job.

No one is going to patrol the streets of a city or go after bombs on rooftops when the air is split asunder with the screams of thousands of bombs hurtling downward. No one is going to try to extinguish incendiary bombs when buildings are being torn apart and are collapsing, when the city is filled with terrible explosions and hurtling steel and flying debris. No one—English or German or American or anyone else—could hope to survive the blast effects and devastation of these bombs.

So the fire service teams, like ordinary civilians, cowered for safety in deep shelters. They stayed away from the streets and rooftops and kept within buildings, because it was suicide to emerge during the height of the attack. And by the time the avalanche from the heavens subsided, it was too late: the incendiaries had already started tens of thousands of fires throughout the entire attacked area.

In the air raids before *Gomorrah* the Germans had suffered heavily, yet could contemplate with satisfaction the superb efforts and results of their firefighting units—both professional teams and civil defense personnel. They realized that the mixture of high explosives and incendiaries would reduce the effectiveness of these forces, but they expected the defense would still play an overwhelming role in preventing major fire spread.

And there lay the crux of the entire matter. *Gomorrah* did not intend to give the Germans a chance, even after the raid was over, to prevent the critical explosive spread of fire. The Germans could not foretell that an almost incredible storm of bombs from the air would hit their nation. But even had the superb Hamburg fire-fighting forces been ten times stronger and more efficient than they actually were, they still would have been totally helpless.

Among the weapons available to the R.A.F. Bomber Command for the "taking out" of Hamburg was the four-pound magnesium bomb. It was familiar enough to the Germans; the Luftwaffe had poured millions of them into British cities. The bomb is a simple tube of magnesium with a thermite igniter. A two-pound head of iron gives the small weapon the force to punch through roofs and floors, and penetrate to the interior of buildings. Then it starts to burn with a violent heat.

Since the penetrating power of the four-pound bomb was not great enough to smash all the way through the German buildings, the British developed two types of bombs of 30 pounds each which would rip clear through four to six stories, and start to burn in the lower floors. The 30-pound "oil bomb" contained a benzole compound and some white phosphorus. The other bomb of the same weight, as well as a 22-pound model, was basically a blowtorch which blazed fiercely and cast a sharp flame from its ignited chemicals.

Because of their method of attack, the British did not know the weight and number of the bombs

9

that actually struck the city of Hamburg; we must turn to the German records for this information. With their characteristic thoroughness the Germans in Hamburg compiled painstaking statistical data on the assaults. For the attacks by both the British and American heavy bombers, they determined that within ten days Hamburg was struck with at least 1,200 land mines. These are very heavy high-explosive bombs that do not detonate upon impact. Rather, they penetrate deeply through buildings or directly into the ground. A timing device sets them off later during the height of fire fighting and rescue operations; or a sensitive fuse is carried, which is detonated by vibration or movement. It was a favorite weapon of the Germans (some of these bombs were still being uncovered twenty years after the war ended), and they received the land mines back with interest.

Between 25,000 and 30,000 heavy high-explosive bombs struck the city. *More than 3,000,000 stick incendiary bombs* swirled down onto Hamburg like raindrops during a cloudburst. A total of 80,000 phosphorus bombs or American 100-pound liquid incendiary bombs were dropped, plus 500 phosphorus canisters and 500 incendiary flares. The official German report on the bombing of Hamburg during the ten days involved states that these figures "are based on a conservative estimate..."

The odds were adding up against Hamburg. The natural building density of the city, its large area, and its vital role in the German war effort all combined to produce natural target selectivity and vulnerability. There were other factors as well, unknown to the Germans and even to the majority of the British bombing crews—one of them a secret new radar device known as H2S, about which we will soon learn more.

And finally, there was the weather. The average humidity for a three-week period plays a major role in the inflammability of a target, since it determines the moisture content of a building and, to a lesser extent, its contents. If the average relative humidity in summer is 75 per cent or more, this serves to increase appreciably the difficulties in starting major conflagrations; the inflammable materials themselves are more difficult to ignite.

This factor, too, was well understood by the British. They knew that if there was a sufficient quantity of combustible material which could be set aflame by the sea of incendiaries—while the high explosives kept the fire services under cover—then the fires could be started simultaneously over a large area. Unfortunately for the citizens of Hamburg, the weather was completely against them.

Between July 1 and 29, the day temperatures in Hamburg reached as high as 90°F., and night temperatures averaged from 47°F. to 86°F.

Early in the month the humidities were high at night; in fact, unusually so. The lowest reading at seven A.M. between July 1 and 24 was 78 per cent, and at nine P.M. it was 56 per cent. Then in the days immediately preceding the attack there occurred an abnormal period of dry weather. On July 21 the humidity reading at two P.M. was 46 per cent. On July 25, following the first heavy attack, it was 46 per

cent, and on July 27, the day before the most successful raid, the humidity dropped to the abnormally low
figure of 30 per cent.

Rain is another factor in fire initiation, spread,
and control, particularly in the eight hours immediately preceding a raid, and the eight hours immediately following. Heavy rains during these periods do
not affect fire ignition and spread within buildings,
but they are very effective in preventing fire spread
from one structure to another. A primary fire-fighting
tactic to halt the rapid spread of flames is not so
much to attack the source of the fire, but rather to
wet down all surfaces exposed directly to the radiation of heat from those buildings that are aflame. If
the walls of buildings are heavily soaked, they are
able to resist fire spread much more effectively, and
they therefore provide time for the organized fire
defenses to act.

Hamburg lacked this additional defense of nature. In the three weeks preceding the ten days of
attack the city had had exactly one and three-quarter
inches of rainfall. The largest amount, one-half inch,
fell on July 22.

And, finally, there is the factor of wind. Until
Gomorrah and the flaming devastation of the city of
Hamburg, the wind was not considered dangerous
unless it reached appreciable velocities. Determined
defensive measures had proved that even the worst
fires could be controlled when the wind velocity
remained below fifteen miles per hour. Above that
figure—from fifteen to thirty miles per hour—experience proved that the rate of fire propagation from

12

building to building increased enormously. A wind of more than thirty miles per hour could turn even a small fire into a conflagration of catastrophic proportion.

On the evening of the first attack there was no wind in Hamburg, only the slightest of breezes. But suddenly all past experience became worthless. For it was the *absence* of any wind that was to create the unparalleled flaming hell in Hamburg.

2

DEFENSE IN HAMBURG

Before *Gomorrah* descended in its blazing fury on Hamburg, the German port had sustained a total of 137 separate air raids since the outbreak of war. The last heavy raid before July of 1943 had occurred a full year before. Since that assault, spurred by minor raids, the city had brought its civil defense organization and facilities to a high degree of proficiency. Indeed, in the light of the utter catastrophe which swept the Hanseatic port, it is surprising to learn that of all the targets on the European continent, the civil defense of Hamburg as carried out through its air protection network, under the Police President of the city, was regarded as the best and most effective in existence.

"The apparent calm from the last heavy raid in July, 1942 until the large-scale raids in July-August, 1943 did not for one moment deceive the responsible authorities who expected heavy raids and considered the greatest possible state of preparations essential," wrote the Police President of Hamburg. "The fate of our cities in the Ruhr district and on the Rhine was a warning. None of the experience gained there was disregarded. The plainly increasing intensity of the war in the air led to an acceleration of tempo in the constant development of air protection measures which finally reached the limit of possibility."

It is safe to say that up until *Gomorrah* the Germans in Hamburg pressed with all their energy to assure that not a single element of their passive defense would be neglected, and that in this endeavor they were successful. No city in the world, not even London with all its experience in air attack, was as thorough or as extensive in its defense measures as the German port. Experts responsible for Hamburg's fire fighting and civil defense activities toured Germany to inspect at firsthand exactly what had happened in other cities which had felt the weight of consistent and heavy aerial attack. Their findings were instituted into law in Hamburg, and all steps taken at once to assure that the lessons would be properly heeded.

Every element of force available in the Hamburg area contributed to the build-up of home defense. The local administration worked hand-in-hand with the Nazi Party, Berlin authorities, and all elements of the armed forces to place at the disposal of the city every defense element when and if it should be needed. In every respect it was total mobilization of all resources, both in manpower and in physical equipment.

Hamburg, like all German cities under Nazi dictatorship, enforced strict laws regarding passive defense measures. There was no problem in recruiting volunteers; everything necessary to defend the city was simply commandeered by the all-powerful police

15

organization. Yet this dictatorial power was not the only basis of Hamburg's exemplary defense structure. The people—from all levels—attacked their problems with great energy. Although suffering the first heavy blows from the air, they still believed in ultimate victory and in their Reichsfuhrer, Hitler.

The most serious problems in creating a civil defense organization arose not from difficulties with the population at large, but rather from the complicated structure of the German government. It is a persistent fallacy that the police state is a panacea for all problems requiring close co-ordination; the police can enforce their rule against the populace, but they are often not so effective against contemporary organizations that also carry heavy influence with the government hierarchy.

Whenever such jurisdictional problems arose, however, the Police President of Hamburg fell back on his strongest recourse, which was the power inherent in the National Socialist Party—the Nazi police organization. In allocating manpower and materiel there were inevitable clashes between the needs of unhindered production and the need to set up fire fighting, rescue, medical, water, decontamination, communications and other passive defense facilities. In the main, though, within the limits posed by the prosecution of the war effort, everything possible was done to prepare Hamburg for assault from the air.

Among the most substantial defensive measures in Hamburg was a major air raid shelter construction program. Under the Extended Self-Protection and Works Air Protection Services, the city assisted its civilians to build shelters in homes and small factories, as well as undertaking the shelter program for hospitals, first aid posts, control rooms, air protection police headquarters, and other buildings and facilities.

This was no simple program, for many of the buildings lacked cellars in which heavy beam and brick or concrete shelters could be built. Hamburg, like many port cities, has a high water table, and in many parts of the city it is impossible to dig down more than three or four feet without finding water.

To meet this critical situation, the shelter program progressed in two phases. The first was to make maximum use of all available cellars and underground areas. All citizens were exhorted—indeed, they were compelled—to shore up beams and roofs, and to provide what is known as "splinter cover" against the blast of exploding bombs and the inevitable flying debris.

As soon as the "splinter cover" program was completed, householders and civil employees went right on working to press the heavy construction phase of the project. All cellars and basements were reinforced with bricks, heavy wooden beams, and concrete. In those areas that lacked underground facilities, the authorities pressed the construction of special splinter-proof buildings, which were mostly underground tubular galleries and circular surface shelters. The design of these latter structures was ideal for wartime conditions, as the use of war materials was kept to a minimum and the simple construction permitted rapid completion of the work. In this fashion, the people of Hamburg received quickly the shelters needed for their protection, and they accomplished this goal without severe financial or labor hardship.

With all "minimum home-shelter" requirements met, Hamburg turned to the problem of additional mass shelters, which could accommodate the refugees from areas bombed out or burned in the incendiary attacks. Special attention was given to rural areas, especially in the Elbe plain. Here the home shelter problem was especially acute, owing to the high level of underground water and the accompanying lack of basements and cellars. To meet the air-raid protection needs, the Germans built many dugouts of concrete and molded bricks. Wherever possible, workers set up special wall breaches to supplement other shelter construction.

As *Gomorrah* approached, the Germans were anxiously at work on improving their entire passive defense system to counter the heavy air attacks they knew must be in store for them—for they had not missed the warnings provided by the thundering air assaults against the cities of the Ruhr. Emergency water supply systems received the highest priority, and all available open water sources were requisitioned by legal command, and utilized to the full. At harbor basins and canals, the Germans built thousands of special ramps, approaches, and platforms. In the rural areas they built water storage installations and dammed streams; all lakes were enlarged, deepened, and cleaned. Suction shafts were dug wherever they might prove necessary. In Outer Alster, Harburg and

Altona, sewers were utilized as conduit pipes from areas of open water.

The suburbs of St. Georg and Barmbeck were the so-called dry districts and especially vulnerable to fire spread. Here three large pressure pipes were built to lead from open water into the closely packed urban area of the towns. In other similar quarters the Germans dug five shallow surface or overflow wells of large capacity, all of which were fitted with stand pipes for rapid connection to fire engines and motor pumps.

Every possible type of water container was requisitioned and utilized. These included swimming pools, water towers, rain water tanks, industrial cooling tanks, all wells, high level containers, fermentation tanks, empty mineral oil tanks, gasometer basins, and even the water channels in the laboratory of the Experimental Ship Construction Institute. All such facilities were equipped as rapidly as possible with special couplings, approaches and suction shafts.

Areas of potential water scarcity were studied, and where nothing could be provided out of natural means, the Germans created emergency water supply facilities. In Blankenese, for example, the cellars of two wrecked buildings were dug deeper, and then converted into water containers. In addition to these air protection police measures, the German military forces in the area embarked on a thorough water supply program, as did all industrial establishments which would have to attend to their own emergency problems.

Experience in other bombed cities established

conclusively that an emergency situation nearly always arose in respect to supplying safe drinking water for the populace during and especially immediately after heavy attacks. The Germans in Hamburg, following a program begun before the war, modified all water mains in order that every main and supply system could be utilized to its fullest.

The authorities catalogued every private well shaft in the city and outlying areas; these numbered more than seven thousand. Fifty-two private wells in industrial and other establishments which provided potable water were converted so that they could be connected immediately to the municipal mains, and thereby supply selected nearby buildings with water. Everywhere in Hamburg full-scale preparations for this emergency were pursued to the limit, and where it was anticipated that normal water delivery means would not suffice in an emergency, the city officials earmarked thirty large water carts for use. These were taken from the breweries, oil works, other industrial establishments, and with the twenty-one carts available to the local administration, they promised to alleviate any foreseeable emergency.

Wherever the police and military authorities decreed, the Germans camouflaged vital targets. These included such areas as the Alster and Lombards bridge, the railway stations, the port for sailing vessels, all wharves, oil depots, and similar facilities. All individual objects which might aid enemy bombardiers in identifying their targets were also camouflaged.

At the beginning of 1943, in order to protect the more important armament works—especially the

The U-Boat Docks

U-boat docks—the Germans brought in powerful smoke-screen generators.

The list of German preparations in the air protection locality of Hamburg is astounding. Every possible source of fire which could be eliminated was stripped away. By order, all attics were cleared of combustible materials. This was not a haphazard voluntary effort, but a matter of law that was strictly enforced and private homes were subject to chance inspections at any time by police officials.

On March 13, 1943, the Commander-in-Chief, German Air Force, issued a general order to Germans in all cities that all superfluous woodwork must be removed from attics. This was done not only to remove obvious fire hazards, but to permit rapid access to any attic or roof area where incendiaries had landed. In all those attics and other building areas where immediate access was not available, the Germans were ordered to construct ladders, manhole entrances, and trapdoors. Again, this was a matter of law, and enforced under penalty of severe fines.

All industrial establishments underwent the most vigorous protective measures. Building roofs were strengthened and often fireproofed. Fire walls between factories were built of brick and mortar to prevent the rapid spread of fire, especially in the port area, where the experience of earlier raids had proven conclusively the effectiveness of such barriers.

Under the broad authority of Section 7 of the First Decree for the Application of the Air Protection Law, the Police President of Hamburg enjoyed extraordinary powers to requisition whatever materials he considered essential in Hamburg's war effort. Beyond the defenses against fire that might destroy structures, the Police President took every possible step to assure that vital raw materials and goods important to military production in the city were confiscated and removed to dispersal areas. The goods were either placed in special fire-resistant buildings,

22

or were moved out of the city altogether, to be used as needed.

It was a wise move. In many instances this procedure not only safeguarded the goods, but also reduced fire hazards and enhanced the survival of nearby structures from fire spread. The official report of the bombing of Hamburg states that as a result of these steps "raw material, food, goods of all kinds, etc., were preserved from destruction in incalculable quantities."

Despite the best efforts of the Germans, however, their dispersal program was not completely successful. Because certain goods had to be available for loading aboard ships at a moment's notice, they could not easily be removed for dispersal and storage. There was also a shortage of manpower, of vehicles, and of motor fuel to accomplish the dispersal program. As the official report stated of one aspect of this problem: "It should also be noted that owing to the exigencies of war, sunflower seeds, other oil seeds, produce, etc., had to be warehoused in Hamburg in unusual quantities, and contrary to the basic regulations in force."

Every public and official building in Hamburg, all combustible woodwork in important buildings, and every shed and warehouse on the quays and wharves, were treated with special chemicals to retard the initiation of fire, and to help prevent fire spread where prompt disposal of incendiaries was impossible. The Germans in Hamburg had begun this program in the spring of 1942, and by June of 1943, about seven weeks before *Gomorrah*, they added to their efforts by initiating a supplementary scheme for the protection of tenement houses on the outskirts of Hamburg, with lime as the protective element. By the time the bombers of *Gomorrah* were ready to leave England for the first attack in the ten-day assault against Hamburg, this program had been completed.

It would be tedious to detail the enormous training program of the air protection police in Hamburg in teaching not only their assigned personnel, but all civilians, every aspect of defense against aerial attack and mass fire. Suffice it to say that under the impetus of the German police state, civil defense training and activities in the city of Hamburg attained an almost unbelievable level of co-ordination and efficiency.

All personnel necessary to a successful passive defense organization—fire watchers, wardens, voluntary firemen, rescue teams, labor gangs, evacuation crews, medical teams, messengers—all these essentials were woven brilliantly into the Hamburg defense system. Nor was it necessary for the Police President of Hamburg to exhort his people to accept the disciplines of a tightly knit air protection community; the British had attended to *that* problem under the severest lash of all—the explosions of bombs and white glaring heat of incendiaries. Not only did the citizens of Hamburg lend their support to the city-wide organization, but they applied themselves wholeheartedly to programs of self-help and neighborly assistance, two lines of reasoning and action which are absolutely indispensable under conditions of mass attack against civilians.

But above all else rose the specter of unchecked flames. Fire, fire, fire—it was dinned and hammered into the minds of the citizens of Hamburg. The police officials, in addition to all the preparations for water supply, set up more than seven hundred large sand-boxes around the city for fighting incendiaries as they fell. In all air raids prior to *Gomorrah*, the self-protection Service of Hamburg was so effective that they dealt successfully with an average of 93 per cent of all incendiaries dropped on the city. On July 26, 1942, the R.A.F. struck in a heavy raid, but failed to achieve a close pattern of bomb drops. One thousand five hundred fires flared up that night and many threatened to spread into major conflagrations; that they did not was a striking testimonial to the efficiency of the permanent and voluntary fire protection services. Their success in combatting this raid made a deep impression throughout the rest of Germany, and the city of Hamburg became established as the outstanding example of the passive defense organization.

Less acceptable to the palate of the western reader, but no less effective in maintaining German morale, was the strict control of the press to assist in self-protection measures. All experiences of air raids *that proved acceptable to the Nazi censors* were published in the local press; here the official report of the Hamburg Police President tells in eloquent fashion the manner in which this ironclad press control was utilized:

"Special value was attached to co-operation with the press so that here too uniformity of control might be preserved and all possibility of doubt of differences of opinion might be avoided. In this way, it was arranged that so-called *Auflagaertikel* (articles issued centrally) by the DNB (German News Service) should not be published in the Hamburg press without previous editing for Hamburg conditions. That it was possible to utilize the great influence of the press for the benefit of the Air Protection Control is greatly due to the sympathetic collaboration of the Reich Propaganda Bureau and the editors of the daily papers. The activities of the press also had a beneficial influence on the air protection discipline of the public."

That Hamburg was *the* city best prepared for any major air attack seems to be beyond question. This fact is essential to the proper telling of this story, for if the flaming catastrophe that swept through the German city were the result of carelessness or stupidity or indifference, meaning might be lost. After all, the flame of a single match, given the opportunity to climb and flower, to spread before a high wind, can gut much of an entire metropolis. But Hamburg had prepared itself for more than three years to meet the very worst that could possibly be expected from the air.

Hamburg thus becomes a lesson, a grim warning, to all the cities in this world today who face an onslaught from the heavens which, at its slightest, would be infinitely more horrible. This is the true meaning of Hamburg.

All the effort and ingenuity of two million people, all the resources of a great modern city, had been marshaled in Hamburg to meet the expected attack. In his official report, the Police President of Hamburg wrote: "...a greater state of readiness in the Air Protection Service was not possible. On the material side—bearing in mind existing conditions—the limit had been reached. On the side of personnel and organization, not only had the legal regulations been fulfilled and even surpassed, but among the entire Hamburg population there was a readiness for defense and a spirit that was bound to surmount any test. Difficulties of a bureaucratic or technical nature, which in a modern state, with a mass of necessary authorities as a rule unavoidable, practically did not arise in Hamburg. Collaboration on all sides, in the spirit of a true National Socialist community, was so exemplary that at least one prerequisite for successfully meeting the severest ordeal by fire was assured..."

During the month of June and right to mid-July of 1943, the Royal Air Force smashed relentlessly at Germany's cities and industrial centers. As daylight came, the growing force of American heavy bombers rose in swarms from the airfields of England and struck again and again at critical targets. The coastlines of Europe shook to the thunder of hundreds of medium bombers and thousands of fighters. The scale of the aerial assaults against Germany was growing in leaps and bounds, but none were so tragic or terrible as the fantastic bombings by the Royal Air Force.

Then came the morning of July 15, and a strange and eerie hush settled over Germany. The silence—the absence of the massed motors droning deeply in the sky—was almost a crash of soundlessness. For several days and nights the skies remained clear, and soon the Germans in cities all across the Reich turned to look wonderingly at one another.

This respite from attack—it was wonderful and it gave one a chance to breathe deeply and to relax. But it was *wrong*, for the bombers were still there.

For ten days and ten nights Germany suffered no attacks. By the tenth day the tension was almost unbearable. It was a frightening suspense.

And with good reason. *Gomorrah* was about to be unleashed ...

3

THE NIGHT WOLVES

By the summer of 1943 the German Air Force was reacting to the British heavy bomber night attacks with all the fury of a wolf pack in full cry after the hunted. At this stage of the war the U.S. Eighth Bomber Command in England was still forced to husband its strength while it waited impatiently for the flood of planes and men to reach full flow. Not so the British, for whom the battle against Germany was already measured by several years, rather than the freshness of months.

The twin-engine bombers—the Wellingtons and Hampdens and Blenheims—were no longer sent on suicidal missions reaching far into Germany. The newer bombers had been spawned. First the heavy, lumbering Stirlings, then the Halifaxes and the Lancasters, great machines designed for one purpose only—to carry massive loads of high explosives and incendiaries to the heart of industrial and urban Germany.

The Luftwaffe recognized quickly enough the threat of such massive bombing attacks, and the major portion of Germany's fighter strength was applied to

Bristol Blenheim

the problem of nocturnal defense against the English
raiders. It was a simple problem of tactics. With all
the energy and the resources at their disposal, the
British accelerated rapidly their campaign to lay
waste not only the German industrial areas, but the
housing, transportation, power, and utilities that sustained the workers in their homes and at their jobs.
Despite all the hue and cry to the contrary, this was
not indiscriminate area bombing in intent, for the
large city areas the British were attempting to oblit-

erate contributed heavily to the war machine that sustained Germany and its armed forces. Unhappily for the strategic campaign, the problems of navigating to a distant city in utter darkness, when targets remained invisible to the eye, when the sky was filled with the prowling "night wolves" of the enemy fighter defense, became so severe that many of the raids were ineffectual because the bombs were scattered over wide areas.

An official report of the Royal Air Force in mid-1943 that assessed the ability of the Bomber Command and its growing strength of superb Lancaster bombers to "take out" the enemy's cities was not a heartening document. Far from viewing the progress of the air war with optimism, it highlighted the extraordinary difficulties of accurate mass bombardment at night, and it warned that the combination of natural obstacles coupled with the Luftwaffe's growing strength in night-fighter forces and tactics did not promise easy attainment of the R.A.F.'s strategic objectives.

At one time—when the war was still new and aerial bombardment was more hit-and-miss than a science—the phrase "bomber's moon" was a favorite cliché of writers who produced rich prose about these nighttime forays into enemy airspace. Indeed, the bomber's moon was vital, for only by such visual reference to aid celestial navigation was there any chance of reaching the proper target.

Then the Germans began to improve their ability to prowl the darkened skies with skill. The gleaming moon that reflected in shimmering streaks off propellers and glistened brilliantly on wingtips, was now a danger. Under the full moon when the entire night sky gleamed in the cold glow, the bomber crews looked toward the sky with more apprehension than appreciation.

Now the Halifaxes and Lancasters and the Stirlings sought the protecting mantle of blackness. Cloudy nights were now preferable in spite of the difficulty of navigation, because a solid cover blacked out the moon, the stars, and even the palest nightglow of the evening sky itself. What nature denied the navigators, the electronic sorcery of the Bomber Command replaced. New radio beams provided accurate tracks in the heavens, and the blacker the skies, the more ample the protection to the raiders.

But soon the darkness was no protection. The scientists of Germany, working around the clock, perfected new radar equipment which gave the fighter planes the advantage of electronic sight. Without these devices, all the searchlights and massed anti-aircraft batteries would have been of no avail to protect the cities. All the guns the Germans could manufacture would not bring down enough bombers to make the British losses prohibitive. Night fighters were the only answer, and to be effective the fighters must have radar senses.

Without radar the night wolves were blind. They groped in the darkness feebly. They could be directed by the giant ground radar sets to the general area of the bombers' path, but the vectoring maneuvers were largely ineffective unless the fighters carried their own means of closing in to the range where their cannon would be effective. Until radar made its appearance on a mass scale within the Messerschmitts and Junkers and Dorniers, night interception would remain a hit-or-miss affair, and the cities would burn to the ground.

A pilot in absolute darkness, knowing that bombers are nearby, cannot rely upon his eyes to detect his target—night interception is just not that simple. He needs close-in direction. Many of the German fighters without radar actually sought not the British raiders, but the invisible trail they left in the skies—a long stream of wake turbulence, air that swirls and eddies in a powerful disturbance for miles behind the cruising bombers.

The sign was unmissable in calm air. If the fighter was far behind the bomber the effect might be nothing more than a sudden light shock, similar to normal turbulence. But if the airplane was close, then the fighter pitched up wildly, or was thrown into a vertical bank. This was the signal, unseen but infallible, that bombers were nearby. The contest took on new significance between hunter and hunted when the German scientists rushed to install new Lichtenstein equipment aboard the fighters. The Li radar, as it was known to the aircrews, gave the fighters what they needed desperately—an electronic night vision. In the nose of the fighter plane was a long antenna, which the pilots promptly dubbed "barbed wire." The field covered by the antenna extended thirty degrees above and below, and sixty degrees to port and starboard. With the Li, the fighter crew could "see" their targets over a range of fifteen hundred to four thousand yards.

Behind the pilot, the radio operator who handled the radar equipment had three screens before him to study and evaluate. It was not the easiest task on his eyes, for the cathode ray tubes used in the equipment emitted a pale blue flickering light, and after thirty minutes of sustained scanning the operator was unable to identify the brightest stars on a clear night. But he didn't have to study the stars—he was actually the eyes of the pilot up front.

What if the target should be not a British bomber, but another night fighter on the prowl? The question was important, since as many as three to four hundred fighters might be in the air at the same time. Into each German airplane went a transmitter that broadcast a special electronic identification signal which, in complete darkness, immediately marked the invisible target—seen as no more than a blip on a scope—as friendly.

The system employed for interception was simple and effective. Ground stations recorded the path of the bomber force across Germany and gave the fighter pilots and radar operators running reports of the bomber positions. On open radio channels they vectored the fighters from their fields on courses to intercept the bombers. When the radar operator was close enough to recognize a blip on his scope, the fighter was free from ground vectoring, and closed in as accurately and rapidly as the radar screens would allow.

All across Germany and in the occupied countries a vast network permitted the fighters to operate with outstanding flexibility. Whenever a fighter was in trouble or had to land at once, airfields held in contact through open lines were alerted immediately to turn on all landing lights to receive the fighter. This procedure not only saved many crippled planes, but enabled fighters which had made early interceptions to land for fuel and more ammunition, and return to the air in time to catch the bombers as they flew back toward England.

Late in 1942 there were enough radar sets installed in fighter squadrons to permit the first mass use of the new apparatus. All units so equipped and scheduled for interception received from German Air Force headquarters the following message:

"Various squadrons of night fighters equipped with the new radar will take off in close formation against the enemy. Shortly before the start the crews will be given the position of the enemy bomber stream and assemble over the beacon on the coast flashing the code signal *Li*. From this point onward they will be introduced into the British bomber stream, which must be decimated before it approaches the target. Each crew is to pursue the enemy to the last drop of fuel."

By mid-1943 not only had the airborne radar equipment effectively torn to shreds the opaque covering of the night, but the Germans were achieving unusual standards of efficiency in the use of their night fighters. Through 1941 and 1942 the Luftwaffe

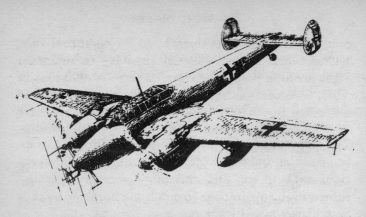

Me-110 Night Fighter

had experimented heavily with their two standard night fighters, the familiar Messerschmitt Me-110 and the Junkers Ju-88.

The Me-110, designed originally as a long-range, twin-engine fighter escort for bombers, had been cut to pieces by the agile British Spitfires in the defense of England. Having failed miserably in its originally projected role, it was relegated to the assignment of bomber destroyer in both daylight and nighttime interceptions. And as a night fighter the Me-110 was a superb machine.

It was fast, easy to maneuver, and had an outstanding rate of climb for so heavy a machine. Owing to the fact that it had already been in production for several years when its need as a night fighter became critical, the Germans had all the advantages of an immediate force-in-being, which they used for everything it was worth.

The one basic disadvantage of the Me-110, however, did limit its effectiveness in its nocturnal role. The airplane lacked the fuel capacity to maintain flight for long periods of time—a serious weakness in night interception and pursuit, when it was often necessary for the fighters to seek out the bombers over long distances for several hours of cruising, engage in combat, and then fly to an airfield.

In time this single fault was found to be so severe that the Germans leaned heavily to the Junkers Ju-88 twin-engine light bomber, an aircraft that ranks as one of the most amazing and versatile machines of the war. The Ju-88 was adapted for light and medium bombing, as a dive and torpedo bomber, as a daylight destroyer against American heavy bombers, and as an extraordinarily effective night fighter against the planes of the Bomber Command.

The Junkers was slower, and it lacked the fine sensitivity to control and the agility of the lighter Me-110, but it could fly with a maximum combat load for at least five hours. Thus it was able to manage the prolonged pursuit so necessary for its night interception mission. To adapt the bomber to its fighter category engineers severely modified the airplane; they did this so drastically and so often that the machine suffered in its handling characteristics and quickly earned a steady stream of curses from its pilots.

Then came sustained experience in combat, and the men agreed that the advantages of the Ju-88 night fighter greatly outweighed its faults. The Me-110 was formidably armed with two 20-mm. cannon and four machine guns clustered in the nose, but the larger Ju-88 not only carried from four to six cannon in the nose, but featured cannon mounted at an angle to fire upwards into the belly of a bomber.

The Ju-88 was a deadly opponent, and in the hands of the skilled and veteran pilots, it became one of the most effective night fighters in the world, and the bane of the R.A.F. Bomber Command.

"It was easy to approach the big British bombers unseen," stated *Oberleutnant* Fritz Brandt, "as we nearly always came in from below, where it was dark. The bombers attempted to evade us by corkscrewing but we fighters stayed on their tails and flew in the same manner."

"We always had the feeling that our task was worth while," explained *Unteroffizier* Ulrich Hutze. "We thought its success depended only on sufficient men and enough fuel. The night fighters came out of the dark like Indians and we always had a feeling of superiority."

All this was true enough, and by July of 1943 the British faced the awesome opposition of some 550 night fighter pilots and their crews, who hunted with deadly skill in Germany's night skies. On an all-out interception with every serviceable machine, the Luftwaffe might put up as many as 400 fighter planes to rush into the path of the bombers—a force that could break the back of the Bomber Command.

Gomorrah depended for its success upon a series of attacks. If the Germans were determined to cripple the bombing effort, they might—with their heavy

Ju-88 Night Fighter

forces and radar apparatus—doom the project to "take out" Hamburg to failure.

But what the Germans could not know was that *Gomorrah* was much more than another mass attack, or series of attacks. Radar had given the German night fighters electronic eyes. *Gomorrah* was about to blind that vision.

4

GOMORRAH—PLAN OF ATTACK

The first three years of World War II were not a time that veterans of the Royal Air Force Bomber Command wish readily to recall. This was the period—from 1941 to 1943—when Bomber Command's overwhelming priority was to build up its strength to the point where it might exert a damaging effect upon the German war machine. It was hardly an auspicious time, for it required a full three years from the outbreak of hostilities before the Command acquired its first real bombing sinew.

The Royal Air Force considers that its Bomber Command engaged in three major air campaigns between March, 1943, and March, 1944. The first of these great campaigns was the Battle of the Ruhr, which lasted for several months, during which the R.A.F. struggled to increase its bombardment skill and numerical strength.

Before March 5, 1943—the date on which the Battle of the Ruhr was launched with an overwhelming assault against the Krupp works in Essen—Bomber Command lacked a true bomber force to hammer Germany's cities. There had been attacks against targets spread widely throughout Germany, and many large fires were started in the cities bombed; unfortunately, careful photographic reconnaissance revealed that the lack of skill in bombing, the navigational problems encountered, the inability to achieve a concentration of bombs in the close target area, all contributed to results that were disappointing. Some of the raids had proven exceptionally effective, but these instances were the rarity, and in the long run the Germans could easily withstand such infrequent heavy raids.

During this trial-and-error period Bomber Command quietly rejoiced as the real heavyweights of its force, the four-engined Halifaxes and later the Lancasters, joined operational squadrons. With its mounting strength, the R.A.F. decided it was time to embark on a major experiment which, if successful, could revolutionize the entire heavy bombing campaign. The experiment, in May of 1942, was the first thousand-bomber raid against the city of Cologne.

To the distress of the Germans, the historic raid proved even more successful than the British had anticipated. Soon after, Bomber Command repeated its revolutionary assault, this time against the Ruhr and Bremen. The path ahead now lay clear—a refinement of the technique of these three raids could inflict terrible destruction upon German industry.

"Those three attacks demonstrated our ability to handle a great number of aircraft," explains Sir Edward Ellington, Marshal, Royal Air Force, "and proved that not only could such a concentrated attack by twice the normal number of aircraft produce more than twice the normal amount of damage but, because ground defenses were swamped, casualties would not rise in proportion to the numbers engaged. Invaluable lessons were learned for the great attacks which were to come; damage was caused on an unprecedented scale; the number of aircraft which failed to return was about four per cent of the force sent out."

This was the most vital period in the mushrooming growth of Bomber Command. The problem facing the British was how best to use the strength of their truly great and still-growing bombing force. The raids by a thousand bombers could not be continued indefinitely, simply because the drain of successive attacks would be too great upon the Command. That the bombers and crews were available was true enough, but a sustained and successful air war is much more than simply throwing every available airplane and crew at the enemy. The thousand-bomber raids might wreak terrible destruction upon the Germans, but the Royal Air Force could continue on such a scale only by stripping the training organization of its instructors and airplanes—which had filled the necessary gap to accumulate the thousand planes for a single raid. Attacks by a thousand bombers, as a regular program, would have to wait. Build-up of the Bomber Command had to be accomplished despite the transfer of squadrons to the Mediterranean and India and to Coastal Command for submarine patrol and attack.

More important was the carrying capacity of the new four-engine bombers. What a thousand twin-engine planes could accomplish could be exceeded by a force of four-engine raiders less than one-third its size.

The most critical problem of all lay not in the available number of bombers for any single raid, but in the best means of utilizing to its maximum efficiency the strength of a single raid. The British sought desperately for a solution to the problem of finding targets in difficult weather, and hitting those targets accurately and with great concentration of bombs. England's scientists had for several years been working on navigational aids, and some ingenious inventions were now ready for trial.

From this research effort there was born in August of 1942 a force known as the Pathfinders—a *corps d'élite* made up of the most experienced and skillful crews, and using navigational aids which altered drastically the whole technique of bombing in darkness. From the moment of their inception the Pathfinders became the hated target of the German night fighters, for these elusive raiders that rushed ahead of the main bomber forces continued to lead those forces to their targets despite the worst of weather and the most determined of Germany's mighty defenses. Once the Pathfinders were a reality, the bombing offensive began in grim earnest.

The new weapons of the air gave to the British a fearsome bombing armada. First of the four-engined heavy bombers to see action against Germany was the Short Stirling, a massive weight-lifter that was rushed into production. The first Stirling took to the air only weeks before war was declared, and early in

Short Stirling

1941 it began regular operations against Germany. The Stirling weighed nearly forty tons, and despite its bulk and lumbering speed, it struck targets in France, Germany, and Northern Italy, as well as delivering effective blows against the famed Skoda Works in Pilsen, Czechoslovakia.

The Stirling, however, was never considered more than a steppingstone to its successors, the Halifax and Lancaster. This was due to its slow speed, low service ceiling, and an unusual vulnerability to fighters because of blind spots in its defensive fire pattern. As rapidly as replacement could be accomplished, the British moved in Halifaxes and Lancasters, and relegated the Stirlings to lesser bombing roles where the operational restrictions were less severe and fighter resistance was expected to be less intense. Thus by the time *Gomorrah* was instituted, the Stirling was out of the running for this operation.

To the Handley-Page Halifax, the fastest four-engine bomber of the new offensive, went the lion's share of credit for the devastation of the German targets. Early Halifax models had suffered from performance shortcomings and were replaced, as soon as Lancasters could bear some of the bombing mission responsibility, by the Halifax Mark II, which proved to be an outstanding weapon. Able to cruise on long raids with a speed up to 230 miles per hour, the husky bomber met all requirements for speed and altitude, and was able to stow in its capacious bomb bay a load of nearly seven tons.

With the Halifax, the Lancaster became the prime weapon in British attempts to smash the enemy's cities, and was recognized by its creators and the enemy alike as the monarch of the world's night bombers. The Lancaster had clean lines and was unusually fast for a bomber of its size; yet it was designed basically as a heavyweight truck.

Within the limits of safe operation in flight, everything was sacrificed to meet the demand of the heaviest bomb load possible.

In structure the Lancaster resembled nothing so much as a two-level freight car. Of the two uneven decks, the upper accommodated the crew of seven, and the three gun turrets. The belly of the airplane was a 33-foot-long bomb bay. Between the two was a reinforced flattened-out box-beam to act as a spine for the fuselage and to carry the bomb load, suspended directly below. Six and seven ton bomb loads were normal for the Lancaster, which accommodated with

45

ease the true monster bombs of the R.A.F., weighing from six to eleven tons each!

The crews swore by the Lancaster, which was an aircraft unbelievably easy to fly for its size and weight. It was the only bomber of the European war able to climb on two engines, and many returned to base shot to ribbons, staggering through the air on one engine alone.

These were the major weapons of *Gomorrah*—the Halifax and the Lancaster. They were well-blooded in the events that led directly to the campaign against Hamburg. The Battle of the Ruhr was opened on March 5, 1943, and lasted for several months. After many repeated attacks, including the breaching of the Mohne and Eder dams by Lancasters, the production of the Ruhr industrial complex was badly disorganized. "Such destruction was accomplished in eight cities of the greater Ruhr," states an official report of Bomber Command, "each with a population of over 200,000, that they became a liability rather than an asset to the German war effort. Smaller cities in this area, including Mülheim, Krefeld, Aachen, and Remscheid, were also reduced to the same non-productive state."

Gomorrah was opened the night of July 24–25, 1943—exactly one night before the Battle of the Ruhr ended with an attack on Essen. It is most important to note that by contrast with the months-long assault against the Ruhr, "the productive capacity of Hamburg, second largest industrial city in Germany and the enemy's largest port, was eliminated with a suddenness that spread terror throughout Germany." (After

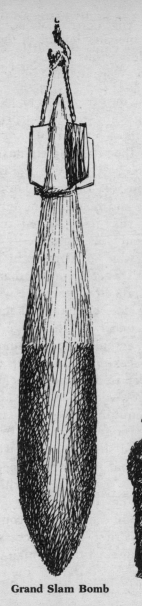

Grand Slam Bomb

47

Gomorrah there came the Battle of Berlin, requiring sixteen major attacks between November 18, 1943 and March 24, 1944.)

But unlike the other campaigns to date, *Gomorrah* was to spring some special surprises on the enemy. One of the most important was the navigational procedure for the attacking Halifaxes and Lancasters. Until this time only a few of the British raiders had carried the new H2S radar, the latest electronic means of identifying and marking the target for the bombers. Unlike earlier navigational and target aids, the H2S equipment was contained entirely within the bomber, and was not dependent upon ground stations. Since it was self-contained and powered by the aircraft itself, its effective range was limited only by the range of the bombers. As far as the raiding aircraft was concerned, the range was absolute.

H2S was actually the forerunner of modern airborne target-seeking and identification radar. Target radar had been under development for several years in England in a variety of forms, but not until 1942 did the H2S equipment begin to evolve. Long experience with the radar gear carried by bombers hunting submarines and ships at sea provided the technical basis for the final H2S arrangement.

The radar scientists learned that objects on the ground or on the surface of the sea would return a distinctive radar echo to the scope observer within the bomber. At first, great success was achieved in the campaign against the German U-boats. Then new experiments revealed that on the surface of the land large buildings, hangars, factories, and other ground objects also returned a radar echo that could be clearly identified against the ground itself.

The implications were obvious, and they promised a revolutionary advance in night bombing and bombing through clouds. Coastlines, rivers, lakes, and built-up areas also returned specific and clearly identifiable echoes, no matter how dark or how thick the clouds.

In its early moments, however, not even the great promise of the H2S equipment could overcome the natural skepticism. Would this electronic "gadgetry" really perform as its proponents claimed? Could cities be bombed accurately by means of radar target-bracketing?

That it was a superb navigational aid lay beyond all question, but even precise navigation is a far cry from accurate bombing of a specific target. Tests continued at an accelerating pace as more equipment was rushed from pilot production lines, and all these tests served only to uphold the promise of the H2S equipment. As more and more sets went into the bombers, the time approached for the first mass test of H2S—and that test, on the giant scale of an all-out bombing campaign, was *Gomorrah*.

If successful, H2S would do more than enable the bombers to find and attack Hamburg. It would enable large numbers of bombers to arrive over the target almost simultaneously; the bomb drops would be more concentrated, and the bombing time could be condensed into the shortest interval possible, turning an ordinary heavy raid into a thundering avalanche of hell from the skies.

An additional benefit was found in making H2S available to the highly skilled crews of the elite Pathfinder Force. On the night of July 24, these Lancasters would sweep out ahead of the main bomber force to find the target. They would dump their special bombs and flares into the exact target areas, bracketing with brilliant lights and fires the parts of the city to be bombed.

Gomorrah was to spring yet another surprise on the Germans. Even the heaviest attacks by Bomber Command to date had been made in the form of a loose, stretched-out formation on a broad front. This was actually an area of air space in which the bombers flowed like loose drops of rain, and as they passed over the target they released their bombs. It was in stark contrast to the American daytime formations in which Fortresses and Liberators flew in tightly-packed defensive boxes of staggered squadrons, designed to

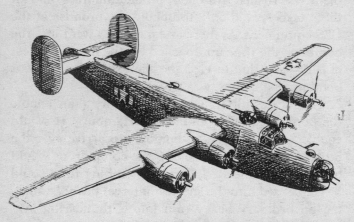

B-24 Liberator

give the bombers the maximum firescreen benefit of thirteen heavy guns per airplane.

If future raids were to be more effective, the British must bring all their bombers over the target in the shortest possible period of time. The effectiveness of a heavy raid soars when there is a concentration in *time and space* of high explosives and incendiary bombs. The mass use of H2S on this raid, as well as the skilled Pathfinder Force, made possible a new tactic, the *bomber stream*.

As the enemy was to discover, the bomber stream provides an unprecedented concentration of attack. The stream was actually a compromise between the loose and stretched-out formation and the tightly-packed daylight formations. Now, for *Gomorrah*, the bombers would approach the target in several waves on small fronts, one wave right behind the other. The Halifaxes and Lancasters were to fly on a synchronized course, altitude, speed, and on rigidly controlled time schedules. Yet they formed no definite formation and only occasionally would two or more planes be in visual contact with one another.

Because of the precise co-ordination of all the bombers, in time and space, the many hundreds of planes would form a stream as the mass approached Hamburg. If all went as planned, the raiders would come over the city in a thick flowing river from three to five miles wide, wave after wave, hurling hundreds of tons of bombs into the city. This unparalleled concentration of explosives and incendiaries was calculated to saturate the defenses of even so well prepared a target as Hamburg.

51

One final hand was to be played this night, and the number of bombers returning would depend largely upon its success. The Battle of the Ruhr had cost the British heavily in losses, despite the widespread selection of targets. Hamburg, however, was a concentrated target, and hundreds of bombers of necessity would have to pass through the same air space. A determined attack by the night fighters could wreak disastrous casualties among the bombers, especially in view of the increased efficiency with which the Li-equipped night fighters operated.

There had been under way for some time in England a determined campaign to stab out the radar eyes of the German night fighters. Despite their unmatched excellence and experience in radar equipment, the British were unable to find a way of "jamming" the Li apparatus. As tests progressed, however, a revolutionary plan began to evolve.

The key to the entire matter lay in the reflective ability of the radar waves. If there was no way to "jam" the apparatus within the fighters, why not use the very operation of the Li radar so that it worked against itself? Therein lay the simple yet brilliant answer the British sought so desperately. Since the radar produced an echo on the scope of the fighter, and the echo was the target—the bomber—why not throw into the air "radar decoys"?

Experiments revealed that tiny strips of metal foil, or even metallized paper, produced an impressive echo on a radar scope. With mounting excitement, the scientists demonstrated that a shower of these tinfoil strips would blanket a radar scope with a fantastic number of echoes, and that each would approximate the echo of a bomber. Indeed, it appeared that enough of these tinfoil strips—given the code name of "Window"—might well throw the entire German radar defense, both on the ground and in the air, into absolute chaos. For not only were the night fighters dependent upon their Li apparatus, but they required vectoring by ground stations to the approximate area of the bombers. Further, the massed anti-aircraft guns and searchlight batteries were also radar controlled. If Window would actually perform as the tests showed, then *Gomorrah* would spring the biggest surprise of all against the Germans by cloaking the bomber stream in a blanket of tinfoil reflections.

The Battle of the Ruhr rushed to its bloody conclusion, and Hamburg moved up a notch to first place on the list of targets. Then came the period of inactivity, the ten days and nights when Germany anxiously scanned an empty sky.

On the evening of July 24, 1943, all Bomber Command crews were read this message from Sir Arthur Harris:

"The Battle of Hamburg cannot be won in a single night. It is estimated that a least ten thousand tons of bombs will have to be dropped to complete the process of elimination. To achieve the maximum effect of air bombardment this city should be subjected to sustained attack. On the first attack a large number of incendiaries are to be carried in order to saturate the Fire Service."

The briefings proceeded in their usual, intimate detail. The crews received specific information on times to report to aircraft, with the time hacks following for starting engines, beginning to taxi, reporting to the runway starting point and finally the exact moment of takeoff for the lead bomber, which would again be confirmed by radio check and signal flare.

Weather for the night was forecast as excellent—good news for the pilots and crews; on previous raids bad weather had killed as many crews as went down over Germany to the fighters and flak.

What about fighters? Again, as on all previous missions, the gunners were given special reports on the disposition of fighter forces, anticipated interception and attack times. Since Window was expected to disrupt both air and ground defenses, all crews were asked to note carefully the reactions of the enemy flak and searchlight batteries, which were also tied in to the German radar network.

There was the matter of Gee—the navigational grids. All navigators would remain after the main briefing for a special briefing to set exactly the invisible electronic pathways along which they would fly.

Some crews would be lost—almost always there are losses. Every veteran of the raids into Germany had heard again and again the story of escape and evasion procedures, but now they listened carefully, for past experience had proved that many men who were capable of initiative and courage had parachuted into Germany and returned. They checked their weapons, their knives, escape maps, European currency—the tools of survival.

Special code signals, radio call signs for the day—it was a familiar briefing, and yet it was not.

54

Most of it had been heard before, but now the words were somehow different; the specific data was certainly different. The briefing was the last chord played in the great prelude to the attack. The next sound would be the deep bass thunder of the thousands of mighty engines roaring their power through the darkness of the English countryside.

Gomorrah was now reality; the Battle of Hamburg was under way.

5

THE FIRST RAID

As the last hours of July 24, 1943 slip into the approaching darkness of the eastern horizon, the crews of nearly eight hundred four-engine heavy bombers walk to their planes. More than five thousand British airmen—pilots and co-pilots, bombardiers and navigators and radiomen and gunners—prepare to turn *Gomorrah* from a paper plan into flaming reality.

The weather this evening is crisp and clean, with excellent visibility. Within the capacious bays of the Lancasters and Halifaxes hang the bombs; fat and squat high-explosive missiles and land mines, incendiaries in clusters and singly, all destined for the city of Hamburg.

Merlin engines cough and rumble, shake through their innards, and then spit great blasts of smoke from the exhausts as the propellers spin faster and faster. The great bombers vibrate with their power. Across the darkening English countryside there reverberates the song of thunder; a satisfying sound to all the veterans of the German blitz who hear the bombers' cry and think of the hell that will be wrought in some German city tonight.

At dozens of airfields there comes the sound of squealing brakes as the Lancasters and Halifaxes taxi slowly on the perimeter tracks of their airfields. Nose to tail, the giants rumble along in elephantine fashion, a procession of death about to take wing. At each field two lines of heavy bombers meet at the head of the active runway; brakes squeal, and are locked. The pilots and co-pilots run the engines one by one to full power, checking magnetos, carburetor and cylinder head temperatures, flaps and trim settings, oil pressures and amperes and hydraulic pressure reading. When they are satisfied as to the operation and the sound and feel of their machines, the engines subside in their great roar and fall back to a massed whispering of idling Merlins.

Then comes the signal for take-off—the rejection of the earth by seven hundred and ninety-one great bombers. Each take-off is a long moment of tension. The bomber stands firmly locked to the runway by her brakes. In the cockpit the pilot slowly and smoothly advances the throttles, adding power, spinning the great blades faster and faster. Then she quivers with the great might of the four motors, anxious to roll. The pilot and co-pilot snap glances at the instruments, and suddenly the brakes are released, the giant is free.

The bomber lunges forward, propellers chewing hungrily at the air, dragging the heavy weight forward. The speed picks up in a steady progression, accelerating as the indicator needle reaches around to forty, fifty, sixty. The tail comes up, there is less drag, and the speed increases even more. Seventy,

Lancaster

eighty...the wings grasp at the air, there is the tugging of lift. With deft touches on the rudder pedals the pilot holds her down the runway, rushing along the paved strip. Then the bomber reaches that instant when lift overcomes the ponderous weight of the machine and its drag through the air. With the gentlest of pressure the yoke comes back in the pilot's hand, the wheels lift slightly from the earth, and the machine of destruction is airborne. She is in her element now.

The wheels come up, lock into place with a dull thud that travels the length of the fuselage. The engine sound is tremendous as the roar smashes into the runway and then the earth, and reflects back again. Then there is even more speed, the wings bank slightly and the machine slides onto her predetermined

58

course. Now the ship is moving fast enough to dismiss the additional lift of the flaps, and the surfaces slide back into the wings, lock into place, and the wing is again clean.

England falls away beneath the bomber, as it does beneath a dozen great bombers, and then several dozen, and soon the figure is more than a hundred...two hundred, four hundred, seven hundred, nearly eight hundred massive machines grimly marching toward Germany. The Channel beckons and the coast of England slides beneath the transparent noses of the bombers, falls away past the wings, and provides a murky view for the tail gunners in their steel and glass cages, surrounded by four .303 calibre machine guns.

It is a good night for flying, and, they all hope,

for bombing. There is majesty in the heavens tonight; the spectacle of eight hundred giants marching in a great river of wings and engines and booming thunder is overwhelming. But through all the feeling of this immense effort, the majesty of flight, there is the grim conviction that some of these men will die tonight, that the sleek lines of the Halifaxes and Lancasters will be punctured and holed and blasted by cannon shells and the crooked slash of flak fragments.

The phalanx of bombers seems almost overwhelming in its strength, indomitable in its sheer number. The opposition, however, is formidable as well; the Germans are skillful and courageous and their equipment is outstanding. They have struck before with terrifying results, and they hope to do the same tonight. But *Gomorrah* still holds hidden its surprises ...

Far ahead of the main bomber force the Pathfinders streak through the skies of occupied Europe, then venture into the heartland of the Reich, rushing along the northern coastline. All told tonight there are 791 bombers in the heavens, but fifty-one of these will not attack Hamburg. Some are assigned diversionary missions, and as the Pathfinders race for the target of Hamburg, the other bombers fan out on their assigned routes.

Along the German defense lines are great *Würzburg* and *Freya* detection and warning stations, and tonight these are a special target for a weapon never used before in Europe. It is an innocuous little thing,

60

the tiny strip of tinfoil, but dropped by the millions in unbelievable locust swarms, the tinfoil is a great monkey wrench jammed into the heart of the German defense effort.

Small British formations race over Holland and Belgium, and strike into western Germany. Along their path of flight the tiny strips of tinfoil flutter through the skies, drifting slowly toward the ground. The main bomber force that rushes toward Hamburg also begins to release its tinfoil cargo, and the result is unprecedented.

On the German radar screens it appears that all of Europe is under a mass invasion of thousands and thousands of bombers. The warning centers are in a state of agitation, and they report, one after the other, that enormous forces of enemy bombers are approaching. They call out cities in the Ruhr as targets, they flash alarms of "hostiles, many" along all points of the coast, the Low Countries, and into Germany itself.

Not only the tinfoil flutters to earth; the bombers split open the night sky with blinding flares, the famous Christmas tree clusters that shatter the darkness with savage brilliance, drifting in sputtering and blinding light. They also drop bombs that scream horribly as they rush toward the earth. All across Germany and in the occupied countries the air raid sirens shriek their warning. Factories shudder to a halt as workers rush for shelter. People clear the streets and hurry into the underground havens, for there is no doubt about it tonight—the radar screens are infallible—Germany is being struck almost everywhere by the greatest armada of bombers ever to leave the British Isles.

The main force of Lancasters and Halifaxes pushes across the North Sea, droning its way into the east, toward Hamburg. Already the Window is having its effect, for even as the bombers move out from England the German defenses are making their moves to smash the bombers. But they will not do so tonight ...

The Pathfinders are well ahead of the initial wave of bombers. Navigators bend to their scopes and instruments like priests at an altar, and with the same religious fervor they call out commands to the pilots. Using their complicated long-range electronic navigational system known as *Gee*, the navigators check at regular intervals the progress of their flight. Each new position is reported to the flight deck as the Lancasters rush toward the unsuspecting city of Hamburg, which for more than a full year has not felt a heavy assault.

Exactly fifteen miles northeast of Heligoland, the Pathfinders—and later the main stream—ease from their established course of flight. The bombers are bracketed in the invisible electronic beams of their navigational systems, and the moment has come to take up a new compass heading. The pilots ease down on rudders and gently move the control yokes. Ailerons and rudders move ever so slightly, and the Lancasters rush directly toward Cuxhaven, seventy-five miles from the target city.

Cuxhaven tonight is especially important, for on the radar screens of the H2S equipment it is clear and sharp and absolutely identifiable, a marker pointing directly at the two million inhabitants of Hamburg. The navigators remain glued to their scopes, staring intently at the clocklike finger of the timebase as it rotates around and around, a perpetual circular movement across the face of the flickering cathode ray tube.

All bombers with H2S move toward their target on the guidepost of the flickering scopes. The navigators see along the very bottom of the cathode tube the first sparkling of green, the shimmering line of the enemy coastline. As the bombers draw nearer and nearer to their target the coastline climbs deliberately up the face of the glass. It is a sparkling electronic echo, a reflection of radiation probing to the earth and back to the bomber in much less than a hundred-thousandth of a second. The coastline slides upward until it stretches across the center of the cathode tube. As it continues to move there appears the first echo-sign of the communities on the land. These are the towns on the coastline and slightly inland, revealed nakedly to the navigators as a series of bright patches of light of varying sizes.

It is almost as if the sky were aligned with invisible guidelines attuned to the marvelous equipment within the bombers. Now the scopes show a serpentine ribbon, dark and seemingly shapeless—the river Elbe, pointing its crooked finger all the way to Hamburg. At first the finger itself lacks definition; it is a wavering blur and the distant city no more than a shapeless, flickering blob on the scopes. But the bombers chew up the distance at several miles

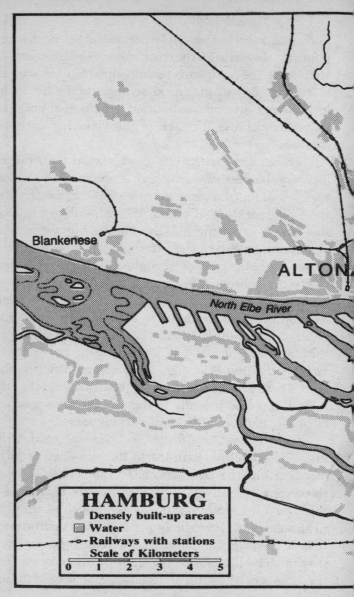

Blankenese

ALTON

North Elbe River

HAMBURG

Densely built-up areas
Water
Railways with stations
Scale of Kilometers

0 1 2 3 4 5

Fuhlsbüttel

Alster River

Alsterdorf

Winter-
hude

Eppendorf

Harves-
tedhe

Eimsbüttel

Rother-
baum

Uhlen-
horst

Alster

Barmbeck

Eilbeck River

WANDSBEK

Eilbeck

Hohen-
felde

H A M B U R G

Hamm

St. Pauli

Neustadt

St.
Georg

Borgfelde

WILHELMSBURG

South Elbe River

HARBURG

65

every minute, and with each passing minute the blur loses its electronic mistiness and begins to resolve into a meaningful pattern.

Bright fingers begin to show clearly from the larger mass; these are the extensions of the docks. Soon all Hamburg can be seen on the scopes, and the river and canals, the major areas that reflect most clearly leap into prominence. This is the electronic introduction, unknown to any of the two million inhabitants below, to the ten days of hell of *Gomorrah*.

There are different impressions with different meanings as the Battle of Hamburg explodes into life. Along the Channel coast the German defense network is a center of wild activity. The command posts of the *Freya* warning apparatus have long before flashed their alert warnings to all the night fighter units assigned to duty, and the Germans are prepared to exact a disastrous toll of the British heavy bombers. There is no question, from the first sightings and alert flashes, that a very large-scale British raid is in the making tonight, and the moment the first definite course of the bombers is reported, the pilots signal their mechanics to close the canopies. The motors of the twin-engine fighters roar as the airplanes trundle down their runways, lift quickly into the dark skies, and disappear into the night.

Each pilot remains in contact with his ground control unit and receives specific vector control—fly to altitude, take up the ordered compass course, additional instructions will be transmitted en route as the planes approach the bombers. But neither the German ground controllers nor the fighter pilots and their radar operators in the Messerschmitts and Junkers know of the incredibly effective diversionary flights or of the millions and millions of tinfoil strips fluttering invisibly down through the black night.

Because of the ground tracking reports that a giant force of hostiles is moving into Holland and Belgium and western Germany, the command centers order the majority of fighters airborne toward Amsterdam, where they will be directed into the armada of the Lancasters and Halifaxes. As the fighters drone through the night, they continue to receive reassuring reports of the progress of the bomber force—unaware that the fluttering tinfoil actually constitutes the bombers.

Then there appear the first cracks in the armor of the German defense. Several pilots call back to their command stations and complain bitterly that they cannot find the enemy; the bombers are assuredly heading in another direction. At one moment a heavy bomber force is reported en masse over Amsterdam and within a minute the ground stations call in excitedly that the bombers are actually somewhere else over the coastline. Hardly does this call finish when another station in great agitation breaks in to report "many hostiles!" west of Brussels, and a few moments later another excited voice shouts over the airwaves that the bombers are actually far out to sea.

With every passing minute the confusion mounts steadily, and before anyone realizes the true situation, Germany is undergoing a deadly crisis. No one knows for certain exactly where the bombers really are. Actually, every radar station on the ground is certain that the bomber force even at that moment is roaring through its defense area. And this, of course, is patently impossible. Yet the flash warnings and the demands for fighters still come over the radio channels in an unbroken stream.

What transforms normal confusion into absolute chaos is that the fighters too are reporting the bombers—in all parts of the Low Countries and over western Germany! Virtually every fighter plane that has been vectored to the reported positions of the bombers is "encountering hostiles," but in a fashion perplexing to the pilots and their radar scope operators. Again this is impossible, but it is happening. From one part of the continent to the other, the pilots report contacts by radar, and that they are closing in rapidly to attack.

In the command stations, the controllers look at one another in complete bewilderment. The pilot reports are consistent—but what they report is absolutely impossible!

The target is picked up on the scope, and the operator gives his orders to the pilot. Fly ten degrees left, climb three hundred feet, bomber dead ahead. The pilots do as they are bid, straining their eyes for a glimpse of the giant four-engine shape they know is ahead of them. But the rate of closure is too swift! It is almost as if the bomber were rushing head-on at the fighter...the scope reports a target from one to two thousand yards out, closing rapidly. It comes down to seven, six, and five hundred yards, and the pilot is prepared to blast loose with heavy cannon and guns.

But at five hundred yards, the target disappears! One instant it is there before the eyes of the operator, a sharp blip on his scope, and the next instant ... it is gone. But there! Again, directly ahead—another Britisher! And again the target closes rapidly, and again it disappears suddenly at five hundred yards.

In the skies this night there is more than one team of pilot and radar operator who argue mightily with each other. Confidence and determination in their maneuvers quickly fade into bewilderment, and all across Germany the ground stations hear the cries of: "I cannot follow any of the hostiles!" and "They are driving us crazy; they are very cunning!"

The precious minutes of bomber interception before the target—wherever it is tonight, the bewildered controllers and pilots have absolutely no idea—are rapidly disappearing. Whatever happens, before long it will be too late to interfere with the smashing of the target, and bombing is rarely so effective as when the raiders are free of the disturbing pursuit and the actual firing runs of the fighters.

Then, suddenly, during a momentary lull in the frenzied and contradictory reports from the ground stations, a voice wild with frustration and rage breaks into the command channel. It is a controller, unquestionably hysterical, who shouts in a shrill voice over and over that "There are a thousand bombers over Hamburg, a thousand of them. They are attacking Hamburg this very instant!" There is no question now of where the bombers are, no question that this is the enigmatic force that has driven the defense system crazy. For now the Germans can *see* the bombers, hear the overwhelming thunder of the massed motors. The Pathfinders have done their task well, and the marker flares and fires within the city are gleaming brightly, a burning candle beckoning to an immense swarm of lethal moths.

By the time most of the fighters respond to the frantic orders to fly to Hamburg at maximum speed, it is too late. The pilots from more than a hundred miles away notice with apprehension the pale flickering glow on the horizon which, as they close the distance to Hamburg, assumes an orange and then an unholy twisting red. When they arrive over the city they are shocked by the sight before their eyes. The earth has been ripped asunder and great crimson flames writhe in agony on the surface...

In Hamburg itself, a war of nerves has been under way since early noon. Exactly at 12:04 P.M. the Air Protection Service receives through the hot-line telephone system the first warning: the city and military authorities are notified of an impending attack within thirty minutes. Nine minutes later, at 12:13 P.M., the warning is repeated, this time with the attack expected within fifteen minutes.

At 12:18 P.M. the sirens scream their chilling sound through the city, and the people rush from their homes and apartments to shelters. Here they remain, waiting in fear for the deep throbbing of the massed motors overhead, the coughing rasp of anti-aircraft batteries. If there are bombers overhead, they know they will be the American Fortresses, for

B-17 Flying Fortress

the British no longer bomb under the sun. But the minutes drag on and on, and the planes do not come. At 12:46 P.M. the all clear signal warbles its welcome cry through Hamburg, and the crowds spill into the hot July afternoon to return either to their jobs or their homes.

Nothing happens for the rest of the day. Darkness settles over the city. Then at 9:15 P.M. the evening quiet in the city offices is disturbed by the frantic ringing of the alert telephone. Air raid expected within fifteen minutes; eight minutes later the sirens scream and the people again rush for shelters. This time they remain underground for only seven minutes, when the sirens signal all clear.

At nineteen minutes past midnight, the hot lines

71

ring shrilly, air raid expected within thirty minutes. Five minutes later, at twenty-four minutes after midnight, the danger signal comes to expect an attack within fifteen minutes.

There is no time to sound the alarm before the terror begins. At thirty-three minutes past midnight, the sirens scream once again. But this time their cry is punctuated with another, far more terrifying roar. The first bombs are already exploding in the city....

The night over Hamburg is sharp and clear, and the people in the darkened city remark with wonder at the brilliance of the stars in the heavens. In the small towns lying beyond the city environs, the crispness of the country air enhances even more the beauty of the celestial vista overhead.

It is not long after midnight that these country and small-town people see an incredible transformation in the sky in the direction of Hamburg. Their first proof of the attack comes as the Pathfinders race for the city, and the flares and incendiary markers spill from the giant bays toward the port. Soon there is increased sound. The deep thunder of hundreds of motors drifts down to earth from a far distance; as the bombers rush in closer the subdued drone becomes a rich throbbing roar and finally a crescendo that beats at the earth in great, smothering waves.

Searchlights flick on suddenly, bright long fingers stabbing in circles into the sky. Moments later the cleanliness of the air vanishes before the volcanic onslaught of hundreds of heavy flak guns. There is the sharp, biting *crack!* as the guns spit intense needles of fire; the sites of the *Grossbatteries* are like forests of living fireneedles stabbing upward. High over the city splotches of red flare into existence; they blossom into angry red-and-black smears, constant brief convulsions of defiance. As the gun bursts increase, the heavens are transformed into a sea of dazzling motes, appearing and vanishing, with new bursts replacing the baleful eyes that wink out. The sound comes to earth as ragged *crumps!* of noise edging through the Gargantuan rumble of motors and the staccato sharp crashes of the guns.

It is a din from Hades, and as the hours pass a new light, more terrifying than anything that has gone before, dances across the horizon of Hamburg, flickering and wavering. Intermittently a tongue of bright red spears upward, clambering for height, to fall back in a dazzling shower of fire motes. As the flames spread, black smoke rises in a mighty column from the city, thick and greasy and choking. Against this ominous background the crimson swirls as it feeds, leaping from building to building, flaring upward.

To these observers the air is alive. From the city the sounds of the exploding bombs are ragged bursts of noise; sometimes the shock waves traverse the miles and pluck with invisible fingers at the clothing of onlookers. It is a terrible sight, and the observers are awed. Against that curtain of undulating blackness the flames belch upward from the earth, rolling and caressing the night air with their terrible touch. From one end of the horizon to the other spreads the growing, wavering light. It is a sight they cannot tear their eyes from, and the knowledge that even as they watch, hundreds of people are burning to death, sinks slowly into and numbs their brains...

Only to the combatants do the sweep of the searchlights and the constant angry crash of antiaircraft shells have special meaning. To the Germans the searchlights and the heavy guns of the flak batteries are next to useless, and they are beside themselves with rage and frustration. To the British, the searchlights which on all previous occasions have been hateful spears of blinding light that bracketed them for attack by explosions of flak, are wonderful testimony to the effectiveness of their secret weapon strung tonight, Window.

Just as the night fighters are crippled—command stations have told pilots that they are entirely on their own and cannot be vectored to the targets—so the ground defenses of Hamburg are thrown into wild and confusing turmoil. Radar, which had proved the electronic strength of the flak batteries and searchlights at Hamburg, now became its direct cause of failure. For both the lights and the guns are radar controlled; tonight, the radar apparatus that sends its commands to the guns and the lights is like a robot gone insane. It reports bombers where they are not, and the searchlights stab helplessly in all directions. "They waved aimlessly in every direction;

it was a beautiful sight to see," reported one of the pilots.

He had good reason to be jubilant, for the lights cannot track and snare the bombers. Instead the lights sweep back and forth in spasmodic jerks, responding to the reflecting echoes of the tinfoil strips in their descent. It is a maddening situation, and just as wild for the gunners. The flak is intense, as it always is over the major targets, but tonight it is badly aimed, and the thousands of shells that scream into the sky are almost wholly ineffective.

The British radio operators who listen in to the fighter command channels, and to the orders screamed by ground command, are thoroughly delighted. The entire defense system is a meaningless, hysterical scramble, and the sounds of frustration and wild rage are music to their ears.

A total of seven hundred and forty Lancasters and Halifaxes smash at Hamburg tonight, and the massive force of four-engine raiders pours a total of 2,396 tons of bombs into the port city. During a period of two and a half hours the high explosive bombs and land mines and the dense shower of incendiaries crash unremittingly into the target. The aiming points for the incredible density of bombs include the suburb of Barnbeck, both banks of the Alster, the suburbs of Hoheluft, Elmsbuttel and Altona, and the Inner City.

Out of this great striking force, only twelve bombers fail to return—twelve out of 740 lost to combinations of mechanical failure, fighters, and antiaircraft.

It is a fantastically low price to pay for what is happening in the city below. . . .

The first raid of the ten days of *Gomorrah* is terrifying to the Germans of Hamburg; they cannot foretell that far worse is in store for them. The picture of the shower of explosives and incendiaries descending on the ground is not far removed from the intended results of the attack. The suburb of Barnbeck is almost wholly destroyed by the vast explosions and resulting fire. The area surrounding Barnbeck on the left bank of the Alster is devastated. A major bomber force in the most effective concentration of the night directs its bombs against the main target, the area on the right bank of the Alster. The suburbs of Hoheluft, Elmsbuttel and Altona, and the Inner City are almost completely destroyed. The port area suffers particularly severe damage. The Germans are unaware of the intended bombing areas, but they have all that night and the next day to determine exactly where the heart of Hamburg is ripped to flaming pieces.

The initial attack reveals to the Germans that nothing previously experienced by Hamburg will compare with what happens tonight. They have no way of knowing of the existence of an attack plan called *Gomorrah*, or that the British have actually launched the opening struggle of the Battle of Hamburg—all this they will learn after ten days, when there is virtually nothing left to bomb in the shattered city.

The British employ new tactics in their bomb drop; this is the result of the outstanding success of the bomber stream. The masses of high explosive and incendiary bombs crash into the target zones in a dense succession of waves. In all previous attacks the pattern of fire ignition was that individual houses in streets and districts burst into flames; tonight, the lessons of earlier experience are shattered. Now it is only the isolated building that is not burning, the lone exception in a vast area torn by blast and fire.

The shower of phosphorus and liquid incendiary bombs is so severe that the fire defenses are completely overwhelmed—exactly as Sir Arthur Harris informed his air crews they must be. Instead of scattered small fires, tonight great conflagrations leap up almost simultaneously throughout the entire area under attack. The high explosive bombs dropped early in the raid score a particularly damaging blow by smashing open the water mains in the most heavily struck area. The Germans who attempt to quench the raging flames face an impossible task, for there is no water, and they watch helplessly as the flames leap unhindered from building to building. And then they cannot even watch, for they must flee or else be trapped by the roaring fires.

It is a grim taste of what is to come; not even the heaviest attack of the previous 137 bombing raids compares remotely to the fantastic carnage that sweeps through the bombed areas. There is noise beyond all comprehension, the continuing explosions of the bombs smashing at the ears and the nerves, stunning the brain, knifing the victims with a dagger of fear that strips them of their will to resist and sends them into spasms of shaking. The flak is a steady, ragged, crashing overhead, and steel splinters sing into the city along with the rain of explosive and incendiary death.

Hamburg is fighting for its life, and the sounds of its defensive struggle contribute to the din—the roar of trucks, motorcycles, and cars, then the cyclonic thunder of the fires, of flames crackling and booming. The bombers are still overhead and their thunder, muted by the overwhelming crescendo of the noise in the city, is only dimly heard. And there are the sounds of the people, shouting and crying, moaning and shrieking in pain and horror. This is the heart-stopping sound of panic, the hoarse animal cry of the terrified that mingles with the guttural commands of the defenders, ordering, working, fighting to save the city.

On this night the Police Presidency suffers several direct hits with high explosive bombs, and then a rain of incendiaries pours into the shattered structure and the immediate area. Fire sweeps through the kindling of the wreckage, unchecked, and within minutes the entire building is a howling sea of flames impossible to extinguish. The control room of the local air protection leader is destroyed by flame from the surrounding office buildings; only by a miracle do the air protection leader and most of his staff escape from the imperiled area in the early hours of the morning.

Thus the passive defense structure of Hamburg receives its initial blows, and suffers heavily. The main headquarters of the police burns to the ground. The control center of the Reich Air Protection League, and most of the command headquarters in the bombed areas vanish in an orgy of flame and smoke. All through the night the weight of the attack and its effects, slowly at first, then with frightening rapidity, overpowers the efforts of the civil defense organizations to rally their strength. Many police officers are ordered out on reconnaissance to bring back personal reports of the situation, because the telephone lines are down and communications have been cut off with many parts of the city. These officers do not soon return, for they are forced to stagger on foot through streets choked with debris, they must make wide detours around great writhing lakes of fire. Not until twelve hours after the Lancasters and Halifaxes leave is it possible even to ascertain what has happened.

Even this first raid, so much less effective than the two major attacks that will follow, plunges Hamburg into terror and flaming carnage. Great fires, born from the wreckage and the sea of incendiaries, rage without hindrance, burning for twenty-four hours before they begin to succumb to the efforts of the exhausted firemen. Supplies of coal and coke stored for the winter in thousands of homes and apartment buildings are set aflame by the fierce caress of the incendiaries. These burn all night, and they will burn for weeks to come.

The fire spread can be reduced or eliminated only by clearing the debris and isolating these buildings and their blazing contents.

The city officials are appalled by the number of dead. In the two and a half hours of the attack, more than fifteen hundred citizens of Hamburg have been killed, a figure beyond belief when compared to even the heaviest of former raids.

The bombs have torn to shreds the main lines of public utilities. Gas, water, and electric mains are entirely out of service and in many cases are so badly wrecked that repair is impossible; the services will have to be rebuilt from the ground up. Early in the attack the high explosive bombs smashed telephone lines; now even underground cables are torn and blasted.

In the docks especially the damage is severe. Wharves and piers are torn to splintered kindling, and heavy fires rage beyond control. All industrial establishments in the area of attack are heavily damaged, some of them so badly they must be razed to the ground for safety.

As the Air Protection Police search through the ruins in the early morning hours they come upon a wasteland of smashed concrete and trees. Twisted steel bars lie in crazy positions, and the bodies of animals and pieces of animals have been flung in every direction. It is the world-famous Hagenbeck menagerie, and it is completely destroyed.

Dawn comes late on the morning of the 25th, and it is a dawn to shock the soul. For despite a bright and shining sun, Hamburg remains hidden beneath a thick yellow mantle that hangs over the city like a dreadful blanket of destruction. Burning piles of coke and coal pour their thick, cloying smoke into the air to drift low over the shattered parts of the city, and the fires still rage in the port area and in the factories with their inflammable contents.

Hamburg has fought well this night, and many buildings hit by incendiaries or threatened by fire are saved from destruction. Yet the weight of the attack, the sheer intensity of bomb concentration, has staggered the people, including the most experienced of the defense teams. The last hope for effective fire fighting vanishes as the water mains fall from a torrent to a small stream, then to a trickle, and finally give out completely. Throughout the attacked area, fires spring up again and again where the teams are convinced all blazes have been extinguished. The flames smolder within the wreckage, or incendiaries come to life again, or the land mines in the very midst of the devastation suddenly erupt with a terrifying roar.

The effects of the raid are so crushing to the city that the Reich Defense Commissioner at once declares a state of immediate assistance for the city of Hamburg, and outside areas begin to marshal forces, supplies, and manpower to assist the stricken metropolis.

Noon comes, and the dreadful yellow atmosphere thickens. Many of the survivors are dazed and in a state of shock; others seem to move with awareness, but their eyes and faces mirror the intensity of the horror they have experienced. Of these people, thousands—with full justification—give up entirely. Dispirited, broken in heart, they begin to wander from the city, missing loved ones, and leaving behind them nothing more than gutted ruins. For them there is no reason to remain in this center of devastation and hell; thus they wander away, not knowing or caring where their steps take them.

They are hardly at the edge of the city when again there sounds the heart-stabbing cry of the sirens. Exactly at forty minutes past two o'clock on the afternoon of July 25, the bombs again begin to fall.

6

FORTRESSES AND MOSQUITOES

In the great aerial bombardment against the German war machine, the Battle of Hamburg was but a phase. The three months preceding operation *Gomorrah* offered few opportunities for the massed bomber forces of the Americans and the British to strike into Germany; heavy clouds and storms obscured the Continent and the home fields of the bombers. The Battle of the Ruhr was pushed as vigorously as possible, but there could be no doubt that the overall air campaign was lagging. Then the murky weather vanished and the two great commands girded their forces for unprecedented blows against Germany. In the history of aerial warfare these were the heaviest and the most continuous air attacks ever known.

The British bombed night after night, setting new records in tonnages hurled into enemy targets. From July 24 to 30 the VIII Bomber Command of the U.S.A.A.F. hammered away in a series of daylight missions without precedent for range of targets, depth of penetration, weight of bombs dropped, number of sorties, and in destruction wreaked against the enemy.

On July 24 the VIII Bomber Command struck at

Martin B-26

targets in Norway, over a range of 1,900 miles. The attack was remarkable not only for the distance flown; it proved to be one of the most precise bombings of the war. On the next day, July 25, the Fortresses of the VIII swung to a new target—Hamburg.

The night of July 24–25, 791 heavy bombers of the R.A.F. struck at Hamburg and swung out in diversionary feints to cripple the enemy defenses. Early the next morning, the dawn of the 25th, a swarm of planes ripped into Europe. American B-26 medium bombers and British light bombers swept over targets in north Holland and northwestern France to draw fighters from a heavy raid by 218 Fortresses on a mission to bomb the Kiel-Hamburg area. It was a costly effort, for determined mass fighter opposition shot down fourteen bombers and heavy antiaircraft fire cost the VIII another five.

Sixty-eight B-17 Fortresses struck heavily against the port, parts of the inner city and the district of Wilhelmsburg with its many valuable industrial installations. "The bombing was spectacular," reports the Royal Air Force in its study of the *Gomorrah* campaign, "and caused severe damage to port establishments and wharves, as well as to sea-going ships and docks." The Germans reported that the damage to residential quarters by the American attack was relatively small, as it was a daylight precision bombing raid directed against specific targets; the latter were struck very badly.

To the citizens of Hamburg the second attack in their ten days of hell was just another raid which fortunately spared them the slaughter of the British area bombings. To the VIII Bomber Command, however, the mission of July 25 had a significant and special meaning; German defenses wiped out an entire B-17 squadron.

On the evening of the 25th, these losses were reported to the interrogating personnel of the 384th Bomb Group at Grafton-Underwood, England. By 7:15 P.M. the debriefing officers were assembled and ready to interview the groups' crews as they returned from Hamburg. Eighteen Flying Fortresses left for the mission, and there would be a total of 180 men to interrogate for combat reports when the heavy bombers returned.

At 7:40 P.M. the men on the ground heard the first surge of engines in the distance; the bombers were coming home....

They were absolutely shot to hell. They were riddled and broken and bleeding. The Germans hit with Messerschmitt Me-109 and Focke-Wulf FW-190 single-engine fighters. Packs of Me-110 and Me-210 twin-engine fighters, as well as Ju-88's, closed to

85

point-blank range and poured withering cannon fire into the B-17 formations. They were raked and cut up and slashed.

At the head of the returning formation was B-17 Number 139, named "Snuffy" by her crew. The airplane was literally a flying wreck, with holes big enough for a man to walk through.

Only ten of the eighteen bombers sent out returned. The story was pieced together in the interrogation room as the crews sipped hot coffee and bit into doughnuts. There had been a savage, running air fight. The Germans swarmed in like hornets as the formations crossed the coast, and they stuck with the bombers, blasting away all the way into the target and most of the way back. For two hours and sixteen minutes the bombers slugged it out with the elite of the Luftwaffe.

The low squadron, the 544th, took the brunt of the fighter runs. Of the seven bombers in the 544th, only one—the "Liberty Bell"—survived the mission. Shortly before the formation reached the initial point where it would swing into its bomb run for the Hanover docks, the last Fortress—"Passes Cancelled"—slid out of formation. The heavy bomber reeled sickly for a long moment, then whipped into a flat spin. She whirled crazily all the way to the ground, and exploded with the full bomb load in a blinding sheet of flame. Only three of the crew were able to bail out; seven men were trapped and they died in the blast.

Over the target the fighters hit "April's Fool" in a dense swarm. She went to flaming pieces in the air,

Me 109G

and only a few chutes opened. The other crews saw the body of the dead co-pilot slumped in his seat.

Then the bombs started spilling through the sky, smashing into the industrial targets, the wharves and docks and the ships. Flame spurted, and smoke boiled up to add to the ghastly pall still drifting from the horror of the night before.

The fighters attacked in wild fury. Three minutes after "April's Fool" shredded in flight, the B-17 known as "Long Horn" dropped out of formation. The bomber was a wreck. The right inboard engine was on fire and trailed thick smoke. The nose of the plane was shot to twisted pieces, and at least one man could be seen sprawled lifeless in the wreckage. The other crews watched in sick horror as a crewman fell from the escape hatch, threshing his arms and legs wildly as he plunged. His chute did not open....

As the stricken Fortress dropped away from the formation the fighters rushed in like sharks, hacking relentlessly with their guns and cannon, making long pursuit curves from the stern, wings and noses ablaze with their weapons. The glass in the bomber's nose and cockpit was all bloody. Finally a man fell away and the white silk of his chute blossomed out full. Two Focke-Wulfs swung around in tight turns and shot the man in the shrouds to gory pulp.

Five minutes after this the "Royal Flush" fell off on a wing and dropped away suddenly. For a moment the bomber hung in a steep curving bank; then, without warning, a blinding explosion ripped through the guts of the bomber. As the metal skin flayed open, the writhing, worm-like forms of the bodies could be seen inside; then the smoke covered everything and only a single body whirled through space. Miraculously, the parachute opened.

Nobody was certain what had happened to the other Fortresses. Three of the B-17's disappeared; no one saw them go down. Just beyond Hamburg the fighters shot away the entire tail assembly of a Fortress; the bomber staggered through the air, with only two-thirds of its body. Six parachutes blossomed. Ten minutes later, its right stabilizer cut cleanly from the airplane, another B-17 gave up its life and went down, winding up into a tight spin. Immediately after that another one went down, one engine flaming, another smoking, and the tail so shot to pieces that daylight showed clearly through the surfaces.

Seven were shot down, and one bomber, completely cut to ribbons, limped its way into a British base, slewed crazily along the runway, and came to a halt, filled with wounded whose blood had collected in dirty pools in the bottom of the fuselage. In another bomber, which landed at Grafton-Underwood, the wounded were lying down as if the Fort were a hospital plane.

Miraculously, the crew of one of the bombers shot down near Hamburg managed to survive. Their B-17 was "Weary Willie," as rugged a fighting machine as was ever built.

"Willie" fought furiously all the way into the target. The crew watched the heavy bombs dropping away and disappearing in sheets of dazzling flame along the docks. Then they got the hell out of there, the fighters clinging grimly and chewing up the B-17. It wasn't long after leaving Hamburg that the ball turret gunner and the tail turret as well ran out of ammunition. Unable to fire, the gunners stayed in their positions and tracked the incoming fighters with empty guns in the hope that they might throw off the German pilots. Well out to sea, with only one other bomber in the low squadron (the "Liberty Bell") the B-17 known affectionately to her crew as "Weary Willie" was about to call it quits.

By all the rulebooks, "Willie" shouldn't even have been in the air. The oxygen supply to the top turret was knocked out. The left wingtip was shattered into a mangled mass of metal. Three engines were hit and smoking badly; then a hornet's nest of 20-mm. cannon shells began exploding in the nose. The blasts hurled the navigator and bombardier back into the tunnel, ripped off their helmets and their oxygen masks. Fragments of steel cut their communication lines and tore their clothing, wounding both men.

89

FW 190

Without oxygen, freezing, and wounded, they fought their way back into the nose in the teeth of a howling gale, grabbed their guns, and continued firing!

"Willie" fell out of formation and the fighters closed in hungrily to deliver the final kill. At one point, with six FW-190's blasting away, the pilot dove in desperation to five thousand feet. During the dive the bombardier was thrown out of the airplane through the top hatch, and the frantic attempts of the crew members nearby to catch him proved hopeless. He was gone.

But not quite! By a miracle he managed to grasp the edge of the fuselage hatch and hung on grimly for his very life. When the Fortress leveled off in a punishing pull-out the bombardier lost his grip and slid back along the top of the fuselage into the open gun hatch of the radio room. He was absolutely stunned by his experience.

The pilot brought "Willie" down to the water in a wild ditching attempt, trying to ease his crippled ship to the surface even as the enraged fighter pilots hammered away. There was more froth and spray from exploding cannon shells than from the impact with the water. The crew scrambled into life rafts and paddled off as fast as they could. Fifty feet from the airplane, they watched their beloved "Willie" lift her tail high and take her last plunge, into a watery grave.

The bigger of the rafts was holed and punctured, and water gurgled in steadily from all the holes. The men bailed and pumped and patched frantically just to stay afloat. For thirty-eight hours they drifted less than sixty miles off the enemy coast. That night they watched the glow in the horizon from the fires still burning in Hamburg, and listened with satisfaction to the deep thunder of the Halifaxes and Lancasters probing into Germany.

Finally a small Danish sailboat picked them up, and the captain agreed to take them within fifty miles of the English coast. They sailed all day, stopping at night because of the mines in the area. At noon the following day a Halifax bomber spotted them and circled low, while the Americans waved wildly and the British airmen waved back. In three hours two air-sea rescue crash boats picked up the crew, gave the Danish captain gasoline and supplies, and bade him farewell. The boats remained in the area the rest of the day and the entire night searching for other fliers reported to be down.

The men returned to Grafton-Underwood; they would fly again.

That night Hamburg felt no bombs, but constant air-raid warnings kept the populace in a tense state and helped to wear down their resistance. Hamburg gained a temporary respite because of unfinished business the Royal Air Force was winding up—the last attack of the Battle of the Ruhr. The Hanseatic port was spared another night of hell because of the necessity to wrap up affairs in Essen, and on the night of July 25–26, a force of 705 Lancasters and Halifaxes smashed the industrial center with 2,032 tons of bombs. The vital Krupp Works suffered terrible punishment, as did the residential areas in the immediate vicinity. Even as Hamburg heard the cries of anguish from its wounded, Essen twisted in agony, the heart of the city seared by an uncontrollable, roaring mass of flame. That night on the Reichsland radio the propaganda minister, Joseph Goebbels, shrieked invective at the British as "sadistic, brutal murderers." Into his private diary, however, went a more realistic notation: "The last raid on Essen caused a complete stoppage of production in the Krupp Works."

On the following morning Doctor Gustav Krupp von Bohlen und Halbach motored to his cherished industrial complex and was confronted with little more than twisted wreckage among which the flames still leaped. The industrialist stared in utter disbelief; his eyes bulged and his jaw fell slack. The good doctor promptly collapsed in a fit from which he was never to recover.

While the British crews slept that day, the Fortresses of the VIII Bomber Command struck again at their industrial targets. On July 26 three hundred bombers left England; of this number a total of 199 struck their targets. Ninety-two Fortresses hit the rubber plant at Hanover, fifty-three bombed targets of opportunity, and fifty-four of the bombers kept things lively in Hamburg.

The first bombs in this second and final daylight attack in the Battle of Hamburg fell exactly at thirty-eight minutes past ten in the morning. The bombs dropped with unbelievable precision into the port and industrial establishments in Harburg and Wilhelmsburg. Especially hard hit was the large Neuhof power works, which the B-17's left an inoperative wreck.

Again the opposition was intense. Sixteen planes went down over Hanover, and eight more fell in the raid against Hamburg and nearby targets. Let one bomber of all those who fought their bloody running air battles with the Luftwaffe represent the others for this day in the mounting assault against Germany.

The navigator: "On their first pass I felt sure they had got us, for there was a terrific explosion overhead and the ship rocked badly. A second later the top turret gunner fell through the hatch and slumped to the floor of my nose compartment. When I got to him I saw that his left arm had been blown off at the shoulder and he was a mass of blood. I first tried to inject some morphine, but the needle was bent and I couldn't get it in. Then I tried to apply a tourniquet, but it was impossible as the arm was off too close to the shoulder. I knew he had to have the right kind of medical treatment as soon as possible and we had almost four hours of flying time ahead of us, so there was no alternative.

"I opened the escape hatch and adjusted the chute for him and placed the ripcord firmly in his right hand. But he must have become excited because he pulled the cord, opening the pilot chute in the updraft. I managed to gather it together and tuck it under his right arm and toppled him into space. I learned somewhat later from our ball-turret gunner that the chute opened O.K. We were at 24,500 feet about twenty-five miles west of Hanover. Our only hope was that he was found and given medical attention immediately."

There was still a wild air battle going on, and the bombardier and navigator rushed back to their guns. Several minutes later the bombs dropped toward the target. Still under heavy attack, the Fortress shook and vibrated from the recoil of its own guns and the pounding of enemy bullets and cannon shells. Several times the navigator attempted to communicate over the interphone system with other crewmen, but received no answer.

"The last I remembered hearing over it was shortly after the first attack when someone was complaining about not getting any oxygen. All this time, except for what I thought to be some violent action, we seemed to be flying O.K. It was two hours later, when we were fifteen minutes out from the enemy coast, that I decided to go up, check with the pilot, and have a look around. I found the pilot slumped in his seat, the back of his head blown off.

"This had happened during the first attack more than two hours before. The co-pilot was flying the plane with one hand and holding the half-dead pilot off the controls with the other..."

Not even the impact of a 20-mm. cannon shell could overcome the tremendous vitality of the pilot. Despite his fatal wounds, he fought desperately to remain in control; his will to fly could not be beaten down so long as a breath of life remained. He was only semiconscious, in terrible pain, and bleeding badly, but he struggled wildly with the strength of a madman at the controls. Big and husky—six feet and 190 pounds—he forced the co-pilot to fight him off constantly. The co-pilot to his right had to struggle to hold him off the control column while the B-17 reeled through the sky in what the navigator and bombardier believed was extreme evasive action against the fighters.

The B-17 was a flying charnel house. In the same attack that wounded the pilot, the top turret gunner had lost his arm. The loss of oxygen to the rest of the crew caused four of the five men in the rear of the airplane to lose consciousness. Except for the nose guns and the ball turret, the B-17 was undefended, and the fighters had a field day. When finally the other crewmen were able to revive the four unconscious men, they were in a terrible state from severe frostbite. All the radio equipment in the airplane was knocked out, and the interphone system was dead.

Not a man in the Air Force would have questioned the co-pilot's decision to turn back at once. His pilot was dying, the top turret gunner was critically wounded and had to be dropped into Germany, four men were unconscious, he had no radio, most of his oxygen system was destroyed, the interphone was dead, and the airplane was shot to ribbons. He did not entertain for long the thought of abandoning the mission; he pressed on toward the target.

The navigator continued: "The co-pilot told me we had to get the pilot out of his seat as the plane couldn't be landed from the co-pilot's seat. The glass on that side was shattered so badly you could barely see out. The co-pilot was operating the controls with one hand and helping me to handle the pilot with the other. We struggled for thirty minutes getting the fatally injured pilot out of his seat and down into the rear of the navigator's compartment, where the bombardier held him from slipping out the open hatch. The pilot died a few hours later..."

The co-pilot shifted seats to the left, and he brought the battered machine all the way back to England. His rank: Flying Officer. His name: John C. Morgan.

The Army Air Forces bestowed upon him the nation's highest award for valor, the Congressional Medal of Honor.

The thickening smoke from the newly struck targets in Hamburg added to the pall hanging over the city. As night fell, many of the people in houses unscathed by the bombs fell under a severe depression. They had not yet been hit, and the blow delivered to Hamburg was not yet so severe that the city would not be able to absorb its effects. But two American raids one after the other...And Essen had been smashed, and the Americans were striking at Kiel and Hanover and other cities. The weather that had been so bad for so long was now perfect for day *and* night operations.

During the afternoon and the evening of July 26, the sirens screamed their warnings of imminent attack three different times—at 1:13 P.M., 1:45 P.M., and 7:35 P.M. The shriek of the sirens sent the populace scurrying to shelter, for there had now been the devastating British attack besides the American raids.

But no bombs fell, and the weary civilians trudged back to their homes or, if they were simply too tired or frightened, they remained in the shelters for the night. It was just as well, for at twenty minutes past midnight, the morning of the 27th, the drone of motors was heard in the distance. The antiaircraft guns shook the city with their cracking blasts, and there was heard the crescendo whistle that only a falling bomb can make.

A terrific explosion resounded through the city, and then, another blast. That was all. Overhead there were Mosquito bombers, the swift and agile British twin-engine raiders that flew the length and breadth of Germany to "keep the Jerries on their toes; sort of muss 'em up a bit." Two bombs fell in Hamburg, but it was enough to shatter chances for rest or sleep the remainder of the night. The Mosquitoes fanned out all across Germany, showing their tails to the Ger-

Mosquito Bomber

man night fighters trying to catch the British planes, but hopeless in their quest because of the hundred mile an hour speed advantage enjoyed by the Mosquitoes.

At 11:45 A.M. on July 27 the public air raid warnings sounded again. At seven minutes past one P.M. their agonizing wail shuddered through the city, and again the populace ran for the shelters, expecting another American daylight raid. But the bombers had business elsewhere, and seven minutes later came the all clear.

The constant warnings frayed the nerves of the people, for at one minute before three P.M. the sirens howled once more; seven minutes later there was heard the all clear.

In the early evening, at 7:30 P.M., the sirens herded the citizens of the city back into their underground caves, where they waited fretfully for forty-two minutes in the approaching darkness.

The people muttered and looked at one another uneasily. It had been too long without something happening, yet Hamburg was obviously receiving the close attention of the enemy. It was too calm, too quiet, their nerves were coming apart. Could it be the calm before the storm?

At twenty minutes before midnight of July 27, Hamburg received its answer. No one could have dreamed in the wildest flight of imagination what was about to happen. Tonight, a city was to be mortally wounded.

7

INFERNO

It begins twenty minutes before midnight; the first dreaded sounds of missiles accelerating in the air reach the ears of tens of thousands of people in the shelters. The drone of motors is overwhelming; the biting crash of flak, and then the first shrill whine of the bombs, growing with terrible speed, becomes an express-train blast as more and more bombs cascade into the air before the first missiles have yet fallen three miles to reach the city.

It is with these sounds that Hamburg begins to die. The target is the large district left of the Alster—Rothenburgcort, Hammerbrook, Hohenfelde, Burgfelde, Hamm, Eilbeck, and parts of Barmbeck and Wandsbeck.

Seven hundred and thirty-nine heavy bombers march through the skies over Hamburg in a bomber stream that is perfection itself. The leading wedge of the phalanx in the heavens has never before been so perfectly co-ordinated in time and space, and the fighters and the flak still lack the means to overcome the effects of Window and the outstanding navigational sensing of the H2S radar. The great river in the air squeezes together, and from the dense-flowing stream of four-engined machines pours an intensity of bombs the like of which the world has never known.

During the night—the fifth attack, and the second of the heavy raids in *Gomorrah*—the Lancasters and Halifaxes of the Royal Air Force dump 2,417 tons of incendiaries, high explosives, and land mines into Hamburg. A great portion of this tonnage drops into the city in a shrieking avalanche in less than fifteen minutes.

The city collapses—in defense, in spirit—before this incredible onslaught. Fifteen minutes after the first bombs smash into Hamburg, the battle is lost.

In the districts attacked the repeated waves of bombers create for a quarter of an hour the effect of a continual rain of bombs. All the terrors of previous attacks are as nothing compared to this particular raid, for the combination of high explosives and incendiaries produces complete devastation.

Fifteen minutes after the attack begins the water mains are shattered. Tremendous explosions tear deep through the street, rupturing the pipelines not only on the main thoroughfares, but along every side street and alley. The water rushes through the mains, spilling uselessly into the craters, and soon even this wasteful flow slows to a trickle and dies out. Communication facilities are destroyed, and those charged with responsibility for the defense system of Hamburg know only that horror is stalking through the city unchecked, beyond all imagination and belief.

Within thirty minutes the entire target area is a mass of flames. Buildings are torn open, walls blown in or collapsed completely, gas mains exposed; the incendiaries continue to shower down, to ignite the material in the wreckage. The area under attack is a lake of tens of thousands of individual fires.

But there is a *second* attack—the latter half of the bomber stream, bunching together as did the first group in order to achieve the unprecedented bomb carpet. Targeted for the second attack are the densely built up and thickly populated districts of Rothenburgscort, Hammerbrook, Burgfelde, and South Hamm, on the left bank of the Alster. It is here that death wields its scythe with the worst fury tonight.

The second target area has a normal population of 427,637 persons—one-fourth of the entire Hamburg populace. This, however, is a prewar figure, and the citizens under attack actually number many more. Industrial workers have crowded into the teeming section, and the influx of homeless persons from the area shattered in the first heavy raid has turned the available living space into a teeming rat's nest. They are all crowded together on this night, and the concentrated bomb drop in a short interval of time subjects them to the very brunt of the assault.

There is a calculated pattern to the bomb drop by the British tonight. The heavy high explosive bombs and land mines fall in a constant rain for fifteen minutes. Almost simultaneously, it seems, the blasts tear off roofs and smash in walls. Doors are blown to splinters, windows vanish in showers of glass. Despite their inner ceilings and walls, the buildings are now unbelievably perfect firetraps—if fires can be started simultaneously. The steel-hard fingers of blast waves have poked and stabbed and stripped so well that when the cloudburst of hundreds of thousands of incendiaries pours into the city, the buildings welcome them in a macabre embrace of blast destruction and newborn fire.

Every type of incendiary rains from the skies— the small, four-pound bombs, the 22-pounders and 30-pounders. There are 100-pound liquid incendiaries, other bombs of 250 pounds, and there are the phosphorus canisters as well. These flood the explosive-blasted area in a smothering, choking rain and present an unsurmountable problem to the Self-Protection Police.

After the initial wave of high explosives and the following rain of incendiaries, the fire-fighting teams rush from their shelters to check the spread of fire at the very outset of the attack. But Hamburg is visited by another wave of the bomber stream, and hardly do the citizens of the city rush from their shelter where they have braved the fury of earthshaking blasts, when the sky erupts once again in a cascade of explosives. The fire fighters have no choice but to dash madly for shelter, or be torn to pieces by the thousands of explosions, the collapsing buildings and the flying debris.

Not all the fires begin to burn quickly and simultaneously. Buildings cut open, their bare ribs exposed, form a perfect forest of material to carry the flame from the incendiaries in a self-sustaining conflagration.

Some of the incendiaries start fires at the top of the houses, others fall through the exposed ceilings into the lower floors. Hundreds of the bombs fall at an angle and tear into the heart of the structures, passing through the space where walls had stood only minutes before. It is the liquid incendiary package, however, which is the most dangerous, for the flaming chemical substances drip down stairs and walls, fall from floor to floor, and within minutes set a building aflame from the very basement to the upper floors.

There is no wind in Hamburg tonight. Paradoxically, the still air is itself a mortal danger. Before a strong wind, the fires would fan quickly into a line of fire, a sweeping wall of flame. But Hamburg is protected by canals and natural firebreaks, and this type of fire is not unknown to the fire-fighting organization and the self-protection units.

But because there is no wind, the flames leap almost straight up with blinding speed, spreading rapidly from floor to floor. Within minutes a building is hopelessly doomed, for the fire has caught tenaciously at its base, gropes its way blindly but with appalling effectiveness through the innards of the structure, and leaps through windows and doors to feed on the wreckage and debris exposed to its greedy touch.

Within thirty minutes of the attack, two out of every three buildings within an area of more than six square miles is alive with the cracking growl of flames about to explode outward. The explosive bombs still fall, scattering even more the blazing phosphorus and liquid incendiaries into areas hitherto untouched. The people who would fight these fires remain in their underground shelters concerned only with the necessity to escape the death that awaits with certainty on street level. There is no water available with which to contain the flames, and by the time the fire-fighting forces emerge from their congested warrens, their efforts will be useless. Even if it were possible to begin some sort of defense, the effort would smother in its own confusion. With all communications smashed it is impossible for central authority to give direction. The most heavily populated area of Hamburg is doomed.

The flames lick hungrily in their thousands of places of birth. Unhindered by either nature or man, they flourish quickly in the vast wreckage of explosively inflammable fuel. The tongues of red and orange leap greedily across the dust and the wood. They snatch at curtains and furniture, at rugs and linen and blankets. Within minutes the room is a mass of flames, and there are thousands and thousands of rooms, and tens of thousands of avenues along which the fire propagates itself.

There is no wind tonight in Hamburg, but this fire makes its own wind, creates its own flues within the heaving ocean of tens of thousands of small fires along which it can travel. The buildings which have been cut open and slashed to their ribs are strange areas of flickering and dancing light, becoming brighter with every passing second. Those buildings untouched by the incendiaries do not remain inviolate for long; they too are about to be assaulted.

Follow the hungry dash of fire to more and more fuel. The incendiaries blaze and sputter, the liquid incendiaries are small rivers of fire, spilling and dropping through cracks and holes and gaping maws in the walls and the ceilings and floors. The flame races along, it jumps and leaps and skips and flings itself from room to room. In the early minutes of the attack the flames become larger, they embrace greater areas, and it is this newborn influx of strength that gives them savage purpose.

The heat from the fire rises quickly, creating drafts of heated air. Fresh oxygen is needed to replace that which is consumed in the flames, and the air responds to the pressure differential. The heat rises, and at the bottoms of the buildings, in the alleys and the smashed ground floors, through the windows that are poked out, the doors blown down, the walls caved in, the air moves. It slides gently at first, no more than the lightest stirring, but it feeds the flames, fresh oxygen to continue the exploding combustion.

The heat within the confined spaces is intense, and the heated gases rise through the available air spaces. As the flames become more intense in the lower parts of the buildings, the fires lift with increasing strength, following the flue of gases. The result is a great series of narrow spears of fire, flaming vines growing out of the fertile soil of combustion and twisting upward.

It is a terrible circle of fire; for as the gases rise and the flames respond, the cooler air rushes in more rapidly to feed the flames at the bottom. The fire area consists mostly of large blocks of tenements in narrow streets. Behind these apartments are terraces, inner courtyards, and small outbuildings. It is these courtyards, which people in previous raids have come to regard as areas of safety, that become the killers of Hamburg. Around them the buildings are pyres of flame three to six stories high, and all life within the courtyards is subjected to a withering blast of radiated heat. Tonight the courtyards are man-traps, and so are the narrow streets through which the flames rush and swirl.

The flames dash along the wreckage-strewn hallways, through the ruptures and tears and ribs of walls, they hurtle through shattered roofs and leap from floor to floor. By now the fires are roaring with even greater strength and the tongues of blazing red leap from roof to roof. They curl and dance and explode violently into the air. They leap into the spaces in the narrow courtyards, and then ... they *join*.

This is the moment of doom. The tens of thousands of individual blazes are spurred on by the force of the rising, heated air. No longer does this fantastic network of flues within the atmosphere rise gently; the air is heated to intense temperatures, and it tries to explode away from the fires. With this increase in rising gases, the flow of air in the streets below becomes visible. It is alive, and it can be seen as dust and smoke travel along with the flow, and the flames begin to bend, making the oxygen-rich river flow faster and faster.

Thousands of fires meet in a fiery embrace above the buildings, and the suction of incoming air they create reaches the force of a gale. Those buildings yet untouched by fire are in greater danger with every passing second. Buildings weakened by fire in their lower floors are collapsing one after the other, spilling flaming wreckage into the streets already crowded with debris. Great showers of sparks boil through the courtyards and the alleys, firebrands and blazing timbers are hurled into areas not yet burning. Cars and trucks left on the streets leak gasoline and other volatile fuel, and in moments this new fuel explodes into flame.

Now the heat is so great that the sheer effect of heat radiation is sufficient to kindle new flames. The heat withers paint and shrivels panels of wood; these start to burn at once. Balls of fire leap upward. From building to building there are created flaming arches, bridges of fire. Everywhere the fire rushes outward, running from itself, a wave of flame spilling and tumbling and crashing blindly in all directions. Overhead, the rising flues of superheated air swirl and bend and spin. The outer edges of the flues touch, create a central column of burning gases to match the hell of the most terrible volcano ever recorded by man. It has not yet reached its full strength, but it rapidly approaches its peak.

Now the thousands of individual fires are combined into hundreds of great blazes that rush to join one another in a fantastic sea of flames more than one and a quarter miles in diameter! The wind has risen to a full, howling gale that draws in superheated gases and fire—for the flames bend in their upward exit through the atmosphere. In the smaller fire areas the flames are fanned as if by an enormous bellows as the central suction of the largest and fiercest fires draws in with increasing velocity the surrounding masses of fresh air. First there are tens of thousands of fires, then thousands, and as the minutes pass the thousands become hundreds. Now, with the fires shrieking beyond all possible hope of control, the hundreds blend into several dozen, and it seems as if the sky over Hamburg itself is beginning to burn.

The disaster that confronts the fire fighters is almost too much for the mind to accept. Dozens of intense flaming areas, each by itself far more than a major catastrophe under normal conditions, are struggling to join one another. When it happens, more than six square miles already subjected to wildfire will be inundated by a vast sea of flame....

Wood-roofed, wood-floored, the buildings in the attacked area are particularly vulnerable to this onslaught of flame, a fire the like of which has never until this moment existed on this earth. Furthermore, the particular manner in which the fire develops arises from the street pattern of the city. Because of the inner courtyards and the narrow streets, the mass of air sucked into the central burning area does not flow from the perimeter of the fire toward the center. Instead, drawn along the surface of the earth, the air must find pathways through streets, courtyards and alleys, through open windows and doors. A screaming draft of cooler air whirls around the perimeter of the great flaming mass in a concentric flow. Although the air flow follows this pattern it eddies wildly to and fro, like a raging rapids turning and twisting back on itself as it follows the course of the main stream.

The current is unbelievably strong, and it explodes from gale force to hurricane winds that lash the fires, sending fantastic horizontal streams of flame along the streets and through the alleys and courtyards. Sparks and firebrands whip crazily through the streets. Whole beams and parts of cornices are aflame. Seized and hurled aloft by the wind, they spread the fire through districts that have previously escaped the flame.

Hamburg is a proud, thriving city of two million souls. It is a city strong and industrious, powerfully knitted together by the common need for defense and the discipline of a police state. But the strength which has availed previously is evaporated in the heat and unbelievable fury of the flames. Hamburg has reached a point where it cannot hope to control the catastrophe which roars and howls in its heart; it is like some great beast thrown on its side to the ground, and it can only lie there, screaming in pain as its attacker gouges out its vitals.

The ascending flames and the total lack of water have completely broken the spirit of the people. They are unaware of the immensity of the disaster which is drowning Hamburg in fire. They can see only what happens in their own sector, but it is far more than enough to extinguish all hope of combatting the shrieking flames. They are obsessed with only one thought—flight, freedom from the savage heat and the merciless flames. But the terraces and courtyards, the narrow streets, these are all blazing cauldrons which have choked off the avenues of escape. Flight that was possible in the first moments of attack, even when the bombs were falling, is now an impossibility. When the heat and the flames make flight imperative, it is too late.

There are many—in fact, the majority—who do not attempt to run from the fires. The air raid wardens, the police, the fire-fighter leaders—people with experience in disaster—find all previous experience useless. They can only rely upon instinct, and human instinct is appallingly inadequate in this moment. They emerge from their shelters where they have cowered for safety, and what greets them is shocking to the soul—fierce blasts of heat hurl them back down the stairs into their underground shelters. Many are smashed down by great roaring tongues of flame that in an instant set afire their clothing and their hair. It is impossible to lead the shelter occupants to safety through this heaving maelstrom of fire, and there is no recourse but to regard the shelter—which as yet provides protection against the flames and the increasing heat—as a place of safety.

They cannot fight the flames, for there is nothing with which to fight. But at the least they can assure the safety of their charges by retreating underground, sealing off the doors and entrances to the flames so that they will not be burned alive. This is what they believe—but when they seal the doors they are sealing their own lives forever, although they do not know this, and because of the manner in which death will come, they never do discover the finality of their act.

Few indeed are the people who are able to escape their warrens and emerge into the streets. And only a terribly small number of these thousands can reach the safety they search for—safety which exists only beyond the flames. The streets and neighborhoods they know so well have vanished. Instead there is only a flaming jungle. Buildings have collapsed, rubble covers sidewalks and streets, a tumbled mass of smashed buildings, blazing debris, and bodies. People who have spent their entire lives in the same neighborhood are stunned by the complete transformation.

They rush blindly down alleys and streets lined with flames. Some of them, by the miracle that spares the small percentage to survive in this ocean of fire, stumble the right way and are able to reach the periphery of the flames before either the fire itself or the fantastic radiated heat condemns them to a brief agony and the blessed oblivion of death. The others—those who hesitate or become confused—rush into areas where the fire is at its worst, and as they run in terror through the blazing gauntlet more buildings come crashing down into the rubble-choked streets, blocking off the last chance for survival.

And this is only the beginning, for the horror of this night has not yet reached its zenith ...

8

FIRESTORM!

This is Hamburg as its first hour of travail this night nears its close. There are no street lights, no power, there is no water, there is no communication with an outside world which seems never to have existed. There is only fire and noise and hell.

There is no light of man, no artificial illumination, yet there is a glare that burns terror deeply into the soul. It spears into the heart of buildings that are drowning in flames, a horrific blending of orange and red and yellow and crimson and white. It is mixed with a terrible dense smoke that boils from the burning buildings.

There is more than dust and smoke and flame, for the combination seems to have gained life of its own. It is alive in its sensuous writhing, the chattering sounds never heard before, the hiss and crackle and the roar. It boils along the ground, a great and terrible creature devouring all before it. The wind is still increasing, until it rivals even the hellish cry of the fire; it is a wind visible in the form of the swirling dust and smoke devils, fierce as a dust storm raging on the open desert.

But there has never been a sandstorm so calamitous as this peak of violence! The buildings collapse in great rumbling tremors as thousands of tons of debris crash to the ground. As the walls give way, they spit fiery remnants in all directions. The sudden crash creates new paths for the wind to explore. Clouds of smoke and dust, sparks and firebrands twist and change in shape and direction; the interruption of flow is only momentary, then the wind howls with increased fury through the blasted streets, scooping up the dark, choking masses and flinging them into walls of Stygian black through which nothing shows. It is a blackness not from this earth, an abyss from mythology and superstition and fear.

Suddenly a deep blinding shaft erupts through the living wall. It licks hungrily at the smoke and dust; for a moment terrified observers stare into an inferno as intense and murderous as those hellish volcanic passages that lead down to the very bowels of the earth.

There now emerges from the thundering masses of fire the creature which is newborn into history. The heat and flues whip the remaining aggregate blazes into a single, all-consuming turbulent ocean of flame. Not a structure within the great rough circle a mile and a quarter in diameter is free of the clutching flame. *Everything burns*. The sea that struggles to escape from its own pressing heat leaps higher and higher, sending up spears of burning gases. With frightening velocity these superheated gases reach into the troposphere, more than forty thousand feet above Hamburg, a pillar of twisting smoke that soars five miles above even the height of the bombers that laid the torch to the city.

This is the moment of the firestorm. A *thing* of pure flame rears high over Hamburg, a fire which has captured an area of almost six square miles, which howls in elemental fury and terrorizes all who are caught in its blinding glare.

All the fires within the target area have joined. There are no longer individual blazes, they have all run together and embraced. All the separate flues have joined in the single towering column of blazing gases and heat.

Where before the cooler ocean of air beyond the fire had tugged gently in response to the pressure differential, it now rushes into Hamburg with insane violence. From all sides the air flows into the clutch of the storm. It moves from far out in the country, it accelerates through the outlying city suburbs, it swirls and flows and rushes and tumbles inward toward the shrieking center. Faster and faster flows the tidal wave of cool air, until there is a hurricane blasting through the outer edges of the city into the flames.

In the suburbs you can feel the steady force of a wind that reaches thirty and forty miles per hour, a strange wind that flows with little variation, broken rarely by sudden gusts. It feels like, it *is*, an ocean spilling toward a whirlpool.

Within ninety minutes of the falling of the first bomb, the trees on the outskirts of Hamburg are losing their leaves. Small branches snap loose and whirl into the current. Dust swirls up from the streets and the yards, and even in these outlying areas you can see the powerful currents of air racing in toward the city.

The fires increase in height and intensity, lighting up the sky for miles around with a dazzling crimson and orange brilliance. It is a light never before seen by a living creature. Hamburg has become a womb for flame, a spawning ground for the fire monster that climbs higher and higher in the heavens. Tens of thousands of observers have gathered at the edge of the city; they see, but cannot believe, what is taking place before their eyes.

They watch a writhing column of flame leaping into the heavens for thousands of feet. It is the fire from which all fear and superstition arises, the wrath of forgotten gods. They watch and they are stunned. The sound is like that of a monstrous, ragged blowtorch. It roars and howls, and interspersed in the deep booming there is a constant, ceaseless crashing, a thousand express trains rushing earthward, cracking open the sky and making the earth tremble. Great spears of flame leap into the sky, giving birth to rich, booming explosions.

Steadily the wind plunging into the fire increases in its intensity. It reaches ninety miles per hour, then a hundred, and still the maniacal flow of air whips itself on to greater fury. It is a tornado, a hurricane, a cyclone and a typhoon all in one, but there is no rain, only fire and smoke and dust and the screaming cry of the storm-whipped flames.

The wind flattens out the flame along the periphery of the central blazing area. It hurls great sheets of fire low across the ground for hundreds and hundreds of feet, searing and engulfing in a fiery caress all within their reach. It spins across streets into empty lots, where men and women and children who have fled their shelters are trapped, and huddle together woefully as the ocean of flames around them dances higher and higher. The blazing sheets boom forth, drowning entirely the shrieks of torment from the doomed. Seconds later the great wave of crimson lifts, and there are no more human beings to be seen. In their place is a lump of smoking flesh, the bodies collapsed one upon the other. There is no escape from this fire.

The winds reach their peak—an incredible storm of flaming air that plunges horizontally through the racked city with a velocity *that exceeds one hundred and fifty miles per hour!*

It is a wind that is twice that of hurricane force. It is a wind unbelievable, a howling force that grasps at trees three feet in diameter and wrests them from the ground by their roots, kindles the wood into flame, and hurls the blazing mass horizontally through the air to the center of the fire, where it is consumed in an instant.

How can you describe the heat in Hamburg tonight? How do you describe temperatures that reach to more than 1400 degrees Fahrenheit? At this temperature lead becomes a bubbling fluid, aluminum has long since run as a liquid. This is a heat so great it explodes wood subjected to its murderous touch. This is the heat that devours human beings and wood and tar and metal and rubber and melts glass. Like the fire from which it is born, it is a killer raging in the heart of the city.

The flames meet and rise. Within two hours after the bombing, the firestorm is full grown. It is too fantastic for the mind to grasp. It must be seen to be believed, and it can be seen only from far beyond the city. For the flames, twisting within a flue of burning gases, reach to fifteen thousand feet above the city. Fire that rears to *three miles above the earth*, a colossus dancing insanely, trampling everything beneath its tread. And above the fire there stretches the plume of gases, struggling even higher, to its peak of forty thousand feet.

As the superheated gases boil upward, they pass through a stratum of cold air hanging thousands of feet above the city. As this happens, the soot and debris in the ascending flue attract moisture. This forms condensation on the countless tiny particles in the rising column, and minutes later, their meteorological reaction becomes visible to the people along the outskirts of the fire. Never before have they known a rainfall such as this one, large, black, greasy raindrops plunging from the sky in an atmospheric rejection of the firestorm sputum.

It is impossible to portray the terror and the flaming violence on the streets, the intensity of the flames, the shrieking fountains and erupting geysers, the colors and the blinding lights, the moments of darkness as suffocating smoke roils out of the glare, extinguishing the light, and as quickly vanishing before an angry wall of new fire. The firestorm howls

118

and thunders with the throats of a billion tormented demons; it is all sound compressed into this mind-stunning roar. And even as the storm gains its strength, it is not enough to drown out the constant crash of more and more bombs and, when the last bomb has fallen, to blanket the thundering roars of the land mines which, buried deep beneath the ground, explode in geysers of flaming debris.

As the minutes pass, the heat radiating from the great fire begins to invade the shelter areas. Many of the people within these shelters had rushed to the streets; faced with an ocean of flame, they quickly retreated to their underground warrens. Not all could come back. Those in shelters yet some distance from the immediate fires often were cruelly deceived. These unfortunate souls attempted to flee, and covered hundreds of feet before they recognized the futility of their actions. Then they tried to return, but they faced doorways barricaded and sealed shut, the terror of the inhabitants forcing them to think of nothing but a shield between themselves and the flames. Those trapped in the streets shrieked and battered vainly at the entrances to these shelters, even as the fire rolled along the streets, whirled around corners, and dipped eagerly into the stairway, consuming the figures that twitched and thrashed about madly as they burned to death.

But now...in thousands of shelters it is impossible to wait any longer. The heat becomes oppressive until it is impossible to breathe, to think, and there is only one overwhelming urge, to flee, to escape the heat, the heat, the terrible, blinding heat! The desperation for freedom from the heat that chokes and blinds them spurs them to rip away their barricades, to pull open the doors, and rush in madness into the streets.

They are doomed. The streets choke in sheets of flame; firebrands and sparks tumble through the air like great glowing eyes. It is impossible to escape these glowing particles. They strike at clothing, at bare skin, they jab into faces and eyes and necks. They stick to clothing like burrs, and at once set the cloth on fire. They are a rainfall sweeping horizontally, and they are maddening. To stop and brush them away is impossible, for then the flames will win, and the stumbling, running people, eyes wide in terror and imminent madness, will meet death on the spot.

Yet they cannot run unhindered, for their eyes are nests of pain and their skin burns and their clothing is aflame. They beat at their hair and faces and eyes and their bodies; they try to slap out the fires already licking upward from their clothing; and their wild dashes through the flaming streets are like the twitching of marionettes. They run and twist, they stagger and stumble and writhe in agony even as they flee, and then they cannot bear any more, and they succumb to the welcome oblivion of total insanity. Some fall to the ground as the fire rushes over their clothes and sets their hair aflame, and the drumming of feet in impossible agony is unfelt and unheard. Others dash crazily in any direction, some of them into the heart of the flames, and perhaps they are the more fortunate, for theirs is a slightly faster exit from the horror and the indescribable pain of flames eating flesh.

Only those who fled in the early stages of the fire had any hopes of reaching safety. Those who remained in the shelters have nothing before them but death. They are forced from their shelters and basements into the streets of fire, and it is not difficult to comprehend that for many, the thin thread of control snaps in an instant. When a man faces the impossible he has little choice but to react either in blind panic or in total mental retreat; it makes little difference, the pain is just as real, the terror as overwhelming, and the inevitable end is the same for one and all.

The sights and the sounds shock these adults into frenzied action. Of the children, what can be said? They are no longer children, they are young animals who share the instinctive terror of any wild creature facing a wall of flame that bears down upon them. Fear is an ocean into which they have fallen and are drowning. For the children and the adults as well, their terror is as water pouring into their lungs and their mouths, it clogs their noses and they cannot breathe. There is nothing in the universe except this fear, this horror. They must flee, they must run. Escape; *escape!*

The flames. Nothing but fire, and more fire. This is a world reduced to fire and noise and pain and burning and a frenzied, shrieking attempt to escape. There is no thought, no reasoning, for it is impossible. They are human beings thrust into the hideous maw of a volcano in full eruption, and what can they do but succumb to the fear that swamps and engulfs them and tears their minds to pieces?

These are the creatures—for in their actions or in the strangling noises that issue from their mouths they are no longer recognizable as human beings—who dash and stagger along streets through which the tar and asphalt run like lava; it *is* a volcano, for the streets are rivers of fire. The buildings burn, the air is alive with flame, the very earth beneath their burning shoes and clothing is aflame. The universe drowns in its fire. These hapless creatures in the strength of their insanity manage to run several hundred feet, or perhaps only twenty or fifty feet, their shoes catch fire and their feet are nothing more than sticks of flame, blazing thin stumps that can no longer support them. They grasp their tortured limbs and crash to the flaming ground, they writhe and thrash madly on the bubbling, burning tar as the fire instantly embraces them in curling tongues, sets aflame their hair and clothes and their skin, rushes into their mouths and burns out the tongues even as they scream soundlessly from throats already blackening, already steaming with the evaporation of the body liquids.

There are in Hamburg this night the large open spaces common to any major city, and it is toward these areas that people flee. There are thousands fortunate enough to escape from shelters not entirely surrounded by tall buildings: the heat is savage and the air filled with firebrands, but at least the streets are passable and the ground itself does not bubble and blaze. These people rush into the hurricane of fire, and because of their momentary success they hope against hope to find a way through the flames. But it is impossible to tell one street from another, nothing can be recognized, and the heat is a constant goad to continued movement. No human being can bring himself to stop and to consider with calculation, in that tidal wave of flame, exactly where he is. He can only run. There is nothing else to do, and hundreds upon hundreds run into the worst of the flames. Before they recognize their mistake doom plunges over them, and they burn to death.

Is there any other way to meet the end in Hamburg tonight? There is, but so precious a means of escape is offered to despairingly few.

Thousands of human beings never have the opportunity. Panic licks at their feet and burns at the edge of their brains, but because they are spared the intimate touch of the flames, because the great roaring fires are blocks away, they retain a knife-edge of sanity in the midst of a world gone mad. They run and run, each breath an inhalation of sweet-hot torture, of superheated air rushing past tongues that quickly swell, down throats that instantly become parched and ragged, and into lungs that seem to explode with the hot, gasping impact. Imagine the horror of those last to die in these groups. They dash wildly, in frenzy, along the open areas, and then a man, or a woman, or perhaps a child—*suddenly bursts into flame!*

There is no fire near them, but there is that terrible incessant, overwhelming heat. Blocks away, a great ball of flame erupts from a stretch of collapsing buildings. The fire explodes its heat outward; the streets are flues, and the heat gushes over the ground. It strikes with visible impact, plucking at clothes, and in an instant a person's entire body is blazing. Hair, clothes, shoes and flesh—all in that same moment—flash into fire, wrapping the staggering bodies in curling flame.

Thousands of people rush for the waterways and the canals that ribbon through Hamburg. Water is the ultimate safety; the brackish, oily, greasy, filthy water promises survival, and like maddened animals they rush to the canals.

Many fail to reach the waterways, cut down by the scythe of fire. Those who survive fling their bodies into the water, stumbling forward until the footing beneath them disappears. The strongest swim to the middle and tread water for hours, dousing themselves constantly to gain relief from the blasting heat of radiation. Those too weak to swim stand on their toes, immersed to their chins, constantly ducking under to gain respite. As they come up again, the heat turns the water on their faces to steam.

Despite their efforts, these people suffer severe burns on their necks and faces. Buried in water up to their chins, they are dying from the heat! They are animals, mindless and unmoving. The heat radiation sucks away their life. The skin blisters and reddens and begins to swell horribly. Their eyes protrude until the bulging is beyond belief. Great water blisters appear and burst unfelt, cascading the bile of ruptured skin along their cheeks and over their open, gasping mouths. Standing thus, they die, their life ebbing away until finally, eyes staring sightlessly, they are swept away by the moving current, lifeless hulks that drift like flotsam along the greasy, heated surface.

It is the children especially who suffer. There are those parents who, through all the vicious terror, keep only the safety of their youngsters in their minds. The children, save the children, oh God, let *them* survive! It is a hopeless urge, a soundless and unheard prayer. There is no God in Hamburg tonight. The parents stand neck deep in the water, holding the children aloft so they can breathe, so they will not drown.

But it is not enough! Their best, the very substance of their heart and their soul—it is all too little. For they must keep raising and lowering the children, plunging them into the water so that the heat radiation will not flay their skins. The children suffer terribly, unable even to cry out, gasping for breath when they are pushed beneath the water, sucking in the terrible heated air when they are thrust upward. Their hair steams. Their tongues are swollen and they cannot cry, they cannot even beg their parents for relief—as if it could be given to them. They can only moan low in their throats, a horrible wordless whimper.

And how long can the fathers and the mothers sustain their efforts? Soon their muscles fail them, their strength flees before the heat and the constant motion. In soundless moments they die. The children ... left in the water, weak, terrified beyond all sanity, thrash wildly in the instinctive reaction against drowning.

As the hours pass, more and more bodies float on the surface, the infants and older children and the parents and the aged. They float, and the heat steams the clothing. Moments later, dried out, the clothes burst into flames. The upper tufts of hair protruding from the water are also afire. The corpses are partially alive with flame. Mostly buried, the exposed skin becomes bloated and bursts open in great watery pimples. The skin shrivels and peels and shows the redness beneath. But at least these dead are beyond physical pain. . . .

Who has been to Hell and has returned, that can describe the ultimate in horror heaped upon horror? There are those in the water who suffer indescribable tortures. They remain standing, constantly dousing their pain-wracked faces and necks. Terror and fatigue exert their toll and finally they lack the strength to perform even this motion of survival. They stand thus in the water, helpless, as firebrands and sparks— so intense that they set aflame and burn to the level of the water thick wooden posts and bollards—sweep into their faces. Blazing sparks stab out their eyes, rush into their open mouths as they gasp for air. Their faces burn, their hair burns, they cannot help themselves. Tortured by the pain, seeking only the oblivion of death, they try to drown themselves.

But nature is tenacious. It has installed an instinct for life in the creatures of our planet, no matter how fierce and painful and terrifying that life may be. Despite their frenzy to die, as the water rushes into their mouths and noses and lungs, they fight madly for life, struggling back to the surface even as tortured minds strive to stay below. It is safe to presume that most of these unfortunate creatures finally lapse into mindlessness before their thrashing comes to its feeble end.

It is thus throughout the sea of fire that tramples Hamburg on this night of ultimate horror. By the thousands the people fall, they suffocate, their bodies explode into flames. Relatives screaming for one another are separated and lost forever. Many of these people wrap themselves in wet blankets or soak their clothes, and by the miracle of being on the edge of the fire, and gaining brief succor from the heat and the flames, they reach safety—their bodies preserved from the lash of flames, their minds scarred forever. If there is any real distance to travel—more than a few blocks—even this desperate measure does not avail, for the heat steams the blankets and the clothes, and soon the very fabric on their bodies explodes into flames and they fall to the ground. The bodies thrash and fling themselves about, the feet drum in agony, hands claw at faces in self-inflicted unknowing pain, and then they are still.

The insanity lasts forever, an unending procession of seconds and minutes, each of which is too much for the mind to withstand. There is a goal to be reached, there is safety along the periphery of the flames. In some areas emergency pipelines have been laid down by the frantic fire-fighting crews, and these men throw into the air a protecting curtain of water. They do not attempt to quench the flames, for the fire in the distance rears thousands of feet over their heads, and such hopes are futile. But the water penetrates some distance into the main avenues, and offers some chance of survival to those still trapped in underground shelters.

It is not only the flames. The wind! The howling, demon-shrieking hurricane is an enemy vicious and alive and incredibly powerful. In the parks men grasp in their terror at thick trees to save themselves from being dragged back into the flames. Who can imagine the terror in their minds as they feel the trees *moving* beneath their bodies, the great trunks lurching as if they were alive, obedient to the demand of the wind?

These hapless souls are like twigs in the blazing hurricane. The howling gusts snatch them from their feet, hurl them through the air screaming, into the waiting abyss. Men, women, children—already burning alive as they are flung into the intense heat, blazing from head to toe before the vast blast furnace of fire consumes life and body in an instant.

As the night passes, many of the narrow canals become jammed with human beings struggling for survival. Behind them are thousands of people also seeking safety, but there is not enough room for all. There is no hope of fleeing further, for the fire looms high on all sides. Only the water is safety. Panic-stricken, the crowd presses forward to the water's edge. The people in the canal, already standing shoulder to shoulder, back to back, face to face, howl and scream at the crowd to remain on shore. As well scream at the flames! They *cannot* stay back; to do so would be to deny the hope of survival to themselves, their families, their loved ones, their children. So they press forward until there is a teeming mass in the water and at the edge of the water.

They plunge into the canal, and their feet strike the heads and faces and shoulders of the people already immersed to their heads. There is not enough room for all, and there takes place in the water— with the inferno of Hell itself as the backdrop—a savage struggle for life. Still they come into the water, suffocating and drowning those unfortunates beneath them. Whenever the firestorm howls anew, or a particularly savage blast of wind and flame shrieks into the mob, it is as though a living thing were injected with a flaming hot needle. The response is immediate and it is horrible.

The struggling mass of people is like a single creature, a monster that writhes along the ground and spills into the water, suffocating the screaming people already in the canal. Soon there are so many jammed shoulder to shoulder, body against body, that they cannot move. They are wet from the neck down, but their faces and their hair steam from the heat. Hair and clothes begin to burn, flames sear their lips and noses. They breathe the fire and the smoke and they choke on the stench of their own burning flesh, because breathing is impossible to avoid after the lungs are emptied and the brain pounds with its need for air.

Wedged together like sticks, they burn and they

die, shrieking and cursing or simply uttering hoarse and meaningless cries. And still the mob presses forward. The bodies sink into the narrow waterway, and feet trample them under. But there are hundreds and hundreds more people, driven to frenzy by the flames pressing closer and closer.

The living and the dead are packed together in a seething mass, a mindless, squirming human-form creature that steams and smokes under the lash of fire. In the shallows, the heaping mound burns with a fiercer flame. There is no rational life in that revolting mass, only things that writhe feebly, that send hoarse and croaking noises from the heat-seared remains of what were once human throats.

This is Hamburg, the ultimate in human savagery. Through the terrible long night human pain, agony, and suffering reach the ultimate. And who can blame the poor creatures who strike blindly at their neighbors? It is one thing to struggle for the survival of the family in moments of distress, but when the catastrophe exceeds comprehension man is driven back to his animal instincts. He fights and struggles only for his own survival.

On this night, as the firestorm howls and booms and thunders, roaring its defiance at the world, there are thousands of individual moments of horror. Children are torn shrieking from their parents' hands by the wind, and flung head over heels, whirling crazily, into the inferno. Adults are bowled over by the wind, smashed bodily with invisible fists of blazing air, hurled to the ground. Their fingers rake bloody furrows in the charred and smoking soil, dig into the softened macadam of the streets. Frantically they attempt to prevent being dragged to incineration, their mouths open, unable to scream, eyes appealing in animal pain. But it is no use against this hurricane that picks up automobiles and trucks and flings them through the air. Entire rooftops, blazing from end to end, rip off buildings and whirl away in turbulent rapids of flame.

Suddenly a monstrous tongue of fire flashes low along the ground, roars hungrily down a side street. A half dozen running figures are caught in the open. The flame does not touch the people, it passes over their heads. But the air is like a wind from a blast furnace. In the next instant the bodies burst into flames.

Tonight there is hope—scant as it is—only for the able-bodied and the miraculously fortunate. The sick and the infirm, the aged—all these are left behind. In rooms and shelters they cower fearfully as the flames roar louder, the heat becomes fiercer. They have been abandoned—but what else was there to do? Fire races through the street at the speed of the wind, and a moment's delay means death for the hale and the infirm alike. The weak must be left behind. The shelters are deep....So they wait, the old and infirm, and unseen by any other eyes they suffer the agony of the damned as the flames strip the clothing from their bodies, sear the wrinkled flesh....

And what of the thousands who do not dare to brave the flames? Sealed into their cellars, huddling behind heavy doors, they have closed themselves off from the outer world and the oceans of fire splashing around and over their warrens.

No flame ever touches them, but not a man, woman, or child survives. Not a single living soul. Not a human being, an animal, not even the smallest rodent, not a single insect, survives the area of the firestorm. In the shelters the heat continues to rise. It becomes oppressive and smothering. The occupants lean back, trying to conserve their strength. Unknown to them, the oxygen they need so badly begins to disappear. These are the most fortunate victims of all, for death comes without pain, in the form of a slow suffocation. They go to sleep, and it is the sleep of the dead. They do not know the moment when their hearts cease to pump blood and oxygen through their bodies.

Others are killed by heat prostration. They lie about listlessly, on benches, tables, and the floor. Families group together, holding hands, or parents embrace the children to quell their terror at the roar and thunder of the firestorm outside. And then, still in this position, they give up their lives, still together, still as a family.

The last soul in the area of the trampling fire giant passes away quietly. Still the heat rises. In the shelters the temperature rises to unbelievable heights without direct flame. Thick glass bottles soften and melt, dissolving into shapeless puddles. Kitchen utensils become pools of molten metal; but no flame ever touches their surface.

There is brick in these shelters. The incredible heat causes the brick to burn slowly, transforming it into a soft ash that collapses slowly under its own weight into a dust-like substance.

Not until many days from now, when the fires are gone and the ruins have cooled sufficiently to allow men to re-enter the hulk that once was a city, will these shelters be opened. There will be other ashes. Mixed in with the melted glass and the dust of bricks and the solidified pools of metal there will be grisly mounds, half-human, half-dust and melted into the general mass of blackened soot and ash.

Thus *Gomorrah* reaps its harvest. The overpowering thing of flame rears high its talons of searing fire, and screams from a billion blazing throats, a sound that crashes in stunning fury through the city and for miles beyond. It is a constant, ceaseless thunder; no man who has heard it will ever forget its awesome, deathly peals.

The fire-thing tramples heavily and greedily on the city. Its claws burrow and rake out every last piece of wood, or of any other substance, that can burn. What it cannot burn, it melts. What it cannot burn or melt, it leaves as blackened rubble, seared and shattered ruins that stand like gravestones in the burning city.

Tonight's horror is not the end of *Gomorrah*. The fire-thing has not yet reached its peak. Only when it can no longer suck from the bowels of the city the nourishment to sustain its fierce energy will it begin to subside.

To the ultimate terror of the survivors, Hamburg is not yet fully stricken. There are great areas still untouched directly by bombs or by the caress of fire. The bombers will return.

9

FLAK BURST

This is the story of one of the raiders that struck at Hamburg; it is told by the pilot of the four-engine bomber. Unlike the American daylight raids in which the bombers flew in massed, tight formations, and events could be reported in great detail, the Lancasters and Halifaxes formed the loose elements of a stream that remained separate from each other. The bombers flew in darkness, they rarely saw other aircraft, and the crew of one plane knew nothing of what happened to the members of another crew. It was a strange and lonely way to fight, and from the historian's point of view this fierce air struggle in the skies has received precious little documentation in respect to the details of these battles. Thus this one episode, told to me one evening by a scarred veteran of the bombing raids as we visited in my den, must suffice for the remainder.

"Usually we could see the cities we were going to hit even when we were miles away. The Germans could black out a city but as long as they moved around, they couldn't hide it. (This is all besides our own navigational fixes and the H2S equipment.) You

Halifax

see, they didn't use many cars for transportation, but all the German cities had trolleys. From miles away we could see the sparks made by the trolley cars. They looked like jagged streaks of lightning and if you knew how to place the light in its perspective, you could accurately judge the distance.

"When the sparks stopped, then we knew that the alarm had sounded and that the people were taking cover. It meant that they had our direction of flight, and everyone was dashing underground. On the second raid—the second heavy raid against Hamburg—we came in so quickly that the bombs were falling even before the people had a chance to get into their shelters. We knew this because we were in sight of the city, and we could see the particular jagged streaks of light from the trolleys.

"On the first raid, I was in a later wave. The city was burning well when we came in sight, and we could see the glow of the fires from a hundred miles off. By the time we moved in to some fifty miles—we were at about 15,000 feet as I remember—it was possible to make out the individual mass fires.

"You really don't see the great sheets of flame when you pass over the city. This always surprised me, and it took some time to get used to the sight of masses of black through which the brilliant fires would show. This was because of the smoke. Directly over the city, there were always thick clouds of smoke that boiled up from the burning areas. Especially if there wasn't a very strong ground wind, the smoke would climb and thicken into a dense mass, and you could hardly see a thing through it.

"In between the smoke clouds you could make out the city. There's a big difference between the great blazes and the incendiary bombs, and when we followed on the earlier waves, we always could tell if the bomb drops were good. The big fires were mostly orange and dull red—especially the latter color, because of the smoke. But the incendiaries were unmistakable. They burned with an absolutely intense light, a really brilliant jewel of flame. If the bomb drop had been good, against the backdrop of the duller, greater fires, would be thousands of these intense burning lights—and we knew from their pattern how effective the raid would be. You could almost always tell right away how it was going.

"The first raid against Hamburg—this was in July of 1943, of course—most of the bombers had passed over by the time we got there. It was murder in the city. I know that the firestorms that came later were terrible and unlike anything that had ever happened, but the fires in the city were as bad as anything I'd ever seen in the whole war so far—and I'd been along on a goodly portion of the major attacks.

"On the second big raid into Hamburg—I missed

the attack against the Krupp works in Essen that was sandwiched in between—I never had the chance to see the firestorm in full strength. Many of the other fellows did, and their stories were almost beyond belief. A few of the Lancs got caught in the flue of superheated air as they passed over the city at 16,000 feet, and it was as if they were nothing more than wood chips in a storm at sea.

"The pilots told me they had no control of their aircraft any longer. They were thrown about by the heat and even flipped over on their backs. Everything sort of went to hell until the Lancs managed to get free of the severe turbulence.

"I didn't see the firestorm, and I nearly never saw another morning, either. This was the last raid I flew for a long time.

"We were at 16,000 feet. Everybody was still tossing Window out of their airplanes, and we howled in glee as we listened in on the Jerry wireless and heard them going crazy. The flak and the searchlights were like the first raid; they waved about aimlessly, and if you caught a packet of flak, it was by the sheer odds of so many aircraft being in the same air space with so much of the stuff.

"We caught it, all right, and there was no warning; nothing. I was flying along, heading for the city, when suddenly there was a brilliant flash. The bomber lunged wildly; it could have been any kind of motion, a violent lurch, a jerk, but it certainly was wicked. Everything disappeared in a second of blinding light, and the next moment, when the shock of

138

the impact left me, I felt a gush of cold air streaming in from under the instrument panel.

"Things really came apart in those moments, to say the least. The blast of wind, and perhaps the uncontrolled motions of the airplane, pushed the oxygen mask over my eyes. I fumbled at it frantically and finally managed to tear it down so that I could see.

"Just a glance at the instruments stopped my heart cold, for the bomber—with all that heavy stuff in its belly—was in a steep right spiral, almost hung up on her wing, and gaining speed with every second. It took me a good six thousand feet to come out of the spiral, to roll into a dive, and pull her out. I kept shouting for the co-pilot to help, but when he didn't respond I concentrated on just saving our lives.

"At ten thousand I had her fairly straight and level, although the wind was no bargain. I yelled at the co-pilot again, but still he didn't answer. When I felt I could trust the ship for a moment, I turned to look at him. His head was well over; he was limp, his head on his chest, and obviously either unconscious or dead. But I didn't know what had happened. Another flak burst that shook us up gave me a bit of light and I saw that the window on the co-pilot's side was blacking out.

"I reached for the flashlight in my flying boot—and almost cried aloud with the pain. That was the first moment that I realized I'd been hit myself. It was a heavy, sharp pain that seemed to be all over my body. Whenever I moved my arms and legs, I felt I'd simply pass out. But there was nothing else to do but fly, and so I did.

"I played the light on the co-pilot, and right then and there I knew that he'd never talk to me or to anyone else again. The window was blacking out from a heavy spray of blood whipping away from the side of the co-pilot's head and his neck; he'd been killed instantly.

"They say that real trouble waits to fall on you like a ton of bricks, and my time seemed to be up. The flight engineer came forward and reported that we had one engine completely gone. Not just knocked out, you see, he meant his words literally. The flak burst tore it right off the wing and threw it away somewhere over Germany. Another engine was losing oil pressure with frightening speed; the oil sprayed back and it looked like we would have fire on our hands in a moment. I feathered this one, and that left me with two engines on one side.

"The flight engineer did the best he could to work with me, then shouted something about an emergency, and he disappeared. I increased the manifold boost to about 54 inches, holding the left wing low.

"We were losing altitude steadily, and Hamburg was almost below us. Funny, never for a moment during all this did we even think of abandoning the bomb run. Just as long as the old girl would fly, we kept right on course. We were real low now, and this actually worked in our favor, as the flak whanged away at the bomber stream well over our heads.

"But the bombs wouldn't let go; the mechanism was all shot up. The engineer went to the bomb bay and fiddled with the gear. He finally ended up stomping on two of the bombs to get them free of their shackles.

"Thank the Lord for all that weight falling away. The moment the bombs let loose the ship reared up her nose, and then settled down in a fairly steady attitude. We were losing height at about 150 feet a minute, but that isn't really too bad, considering that we'd come down this far like a rock. I rolled her into a wide turn and set for home. Even that wasn't any guarantee—for after we left the target and I had the chance to look around, I wasn't at all sure we would make it.

"The first thing I learned was where that draft came from. We had no nose left. The flak burst had ripped away the entire nose section—it was just a big hole up front. As for the navigator—he had been acting as bombardier—he was blown out into space, dead or alive. I've never learned which. It was this mess up front that kept forcing us down. Normally the old bird would fly like an angel on only two engines, but with that fearsome drag she just didn't have it.

"That made a navigator-bombardier lost and most likely dead, and the co-pilot dead as well. The flight engineer came back to report that steel splinters had torn the radio-navigator's hand right off his arm. He'd managed to get a tourniquet on, and it looked as if the boy would live.

"The top-turret gunner, however, had less than a fifty-fifty chance, for his right leg was gone. They'd put a tourniquet on his leg, and used the first-aid kit as best they could, but it was touch and go because of all the blood he'd lost.

"On top of this, most of the instruments were knocked out. The radio was shot to pieces, and that meant all our navigation gear was gone. I had some flight instruments, and that was all. I turned for England almost by instinct, and thank heaven for those fires already flaring up in Hamburg. We—the tail gunner, that is—could see them for more than ninety miles going away, and that gave me the reference I needed for direction. It was a clear night as well, or else we would never have made it home.

"The pain kept getting worse, but there was nothing I could do. Things weren't so bad if I simply sat, but whenever I moved my arms and legs any distance at all, someone slammed a red-hot poker right into my back. There wasn't much use in making any noise about it, though, for if I didn't fly the airplane, who would? And the radio-navigator and the turret gunner couldn't bail out in *their* condition. Besides, no one likes to call it quits when the machine is still flying.

"Over France we were down to three thousand feet, and still giving up our precious height. We made the Channel at just above a thousand feet, and it was a touch-and-go struggle to make it across the water. But make it we did, and I dropped her down at the first field that came into sight, while the flight engineer fired off all the flares he could find.

"When the aircraft rolled to a stop, I couldn't believe we were really back and safe on the ground. I undid the belt and started to get out of my seat; or perhaps I should say that I tried to do all this.

"That was the last I remembered for quite a while. I didn't see any colored lights or a red haze or anything. I just blacked out. When I came to I was in a hospital bed, wrapped almost from head to toe in plaster. It seems I took not only the full force of the flak burst, but got quite a few of its pieces as well.

"The doctors told me I had twenty-three fractures, including three in my spine. No one could explain—least of all myself—how I got that crate home.

"I spent the next fourteen months wrapped up in plaster, and it wasn't until February in 1945 that I was able to get back into combat."

10

COMPLETION OF GOMORRAH

All through the night the fires burn. It is useless to describe the climax of horror, the agony and death that visits tens of thousands of human beings of all ages. What has happened in Hamburg is beyond imagination; compassion overflows, and further attempts to comprehend the full scale of the disaster produce only numbness.

The bombers come again, and again. Shortly before midnight of July 29–30, 726 Lancasters and Halifaxes storm into the air space over Hamburg in the long, flowing bomber stream, and another 2,382 tons of high explosives and incendiaries smash down from the heavens.

The target includes the districts, hitherto spared or suffering only slight damage, of Harvestude, Retherbaum, and Eppendorf on the right bank of the Alster, and St. Georg, Uhlenhorst, Winterhude, and Barmbeck on the left bank. One of the major targets is the storage district in the port area, and the British raiders strike this zone with deadly accuracy, smashing the valuable military supplies and setting the area aflame.

In Barmbeck, one of the most densely built-up and heavily populated districts of the city, what the fires have missed before they do not fail to ignite this evening. The packed apartment buildings, although not suffering the massed firestorm of the preceding raid, are swept by great area fires. The blaze continues through the night and when a sickly dawn penetrates the dense pall of smoke over the city, Barmbeck is finished. It will never be rebuilt; there can only be razing of the gutted ruins and completely new construction.

The casualties this night are far less than they were during the preceding raid, in which a minimum of sixty thousand human beings died. Because of the extensive evacuation—some 900,000 people in all—as well as the tens of thousands who have fled in terror, the casualty list and the number of missing are much smaller.

But there is no relief from the great flaming torch that has been gutting Hamburg. There is no central firestorm tonight, but the attacked districts are swollen with flames—and area fires rage unchecked. Fire fighting proceeds bravely but sporadically, and what successes are achieved are isolated instances in a deluge of thundering flame. Because of these sweeping blazes, the area burned out is at least equal to that of the preceding assault.

By now the defense forces of Hamburg are reeling from the continued bombings. Men have gone without sleep and with little food or water for days. They stumble and stagger as they attempt to fight the flames. More than 800 major breaks in the water

main system still cripple all hopes of gaining sufficient water pressure to maintain a defense. Trucks
and equipment are for the most part destroyed. Roads
in the heavily bombed areas are impassable. There
are shortages of food, water, fuel, and spare parts.
Above all there are not enough skilled and experienced men to save even a small part of the burning
districts. All Hamburg has become one enormous fire
area, and the battle that is to be fought—and has
been waged with absolutely no success on the major
scale—is one encompassing the entire city.

The number of the dead is beyond belief, and
this does not include thousands still listed simply as
"missing." In areas either fringed with fire or suffering sporadic invasion of flames, there is hope to save
the wounded, and to dig out those who are trapped
beneath their shattered buildings. The rescue workers
drive themselves to exhaustion—and still they cannot sleep. They know that if they stop they will be
condemning to death thousands of people who must
be rescued before the flames sweep into their wreckage-
created tombs.

Doctors and nurses and their aides work day and
night to save the injured; often these people have to
pass up administering treatment to the very seriously burned or the badly injured. There is not enough
time to care for all! They must work swiftly, faster
and faster, from body to body to body, from child to
adult to child, struggling to save as many as possible.
The ministrations afforded a man burned terribly
may save his life, but he must be sacrificed or time

will run out for a half-dozen other agonized, suffering souls.

Tens of thousands of men and women struggle in labor gangs to clear the roads and the streets. It is impossible to use construction machinery in most areas, so the thousands of hands suffice. Bricks, concrete, tangled metal—it is all grasped and shoved aside. There are no city streets, only narrow passageways between mounds of rubble.

Trains move into the outskirts of the city, and again the horde of human beings attempting to escape— on their own or under the exhortations of the city officials—numbers in the tens of thousands. Hamburg is drained of its very substance—its people. It is an enormous task, this evacuation of far more than half of the city. The refugees must be housed, cared for, given medical attention, fed, provided with information, kept under control, and as soon as possible, put to work clearing the debris.

For the most part Hamburg is a shattered city. The devastation has stunned both the attackers and the receivers. After the third heavy British attack, only the districts of Fuhlsbuttel, Alsterdorf and Eppendorf, and the suburbs of Harburg, Bergedorf, and the Elbe remain more or less unharmed. The whole of the remaining urban area is either heavily damaged or destroyed. Even in those districts not yet completely devastated—the inner city, for example— only small portions have escaped destruction.

Hamburg is also commercially crippled. There is precious little gas for cooking, water is virtually nonexistent because of the smashed mains, and electric power is available only where by some miracle the bombs and flames have not cut the lines. Most of the power works and generators are in ruins; thus the factories which have escaped the wrath of the flames and the steel fist of the explosive bombs are rendered useless. Moreover, hundreds of thousands of people have fled, and are scattering through the countryside. Even the vital military industries, which have the means to supply their own power from private generators, are mainly shut down. There are too few workers to man the machines.

The fourth and final heavy raid of *Gomorrah* begins the evening of August 2. Fortunately for the Germans in the shattered hulk of the city, the weather finally takes a turn for the worse, and what would be normally regarded as severe and unpleasant storms become an unexpected and welcome respite from continued mass horror.

In the three major attacks to date the Bomber Command of the Royal Air Force has suffered a loss of 57 heavy bombers. This is 2.4 per cent of all sorties flown—a striking testimony to the effectiveness of bomber stream and the innovations of Window and H2S; on all previous attacks against Hamburg the British have lost more than six per cent of their raiding forces. On the final attack, however, not only do the Germans escape with little damage—although several hundred people are killed and hundreds of individual fires started—but Bomber Command suffers its worst losses. Thirty bombers are lost, and this is 4.1 per cent of the force that takes off from England.

German defenses are not the cause, however. Weather is the killer. All the day of August 2, England is lashed by severe thunderstorms. Lightning flashes dangerously through the skies, and from the cumulonimbus clouds that tower thousands of feet over the British Isles, torrential rains inundate the cities and the countryside. The crews of the Lincolnshire fields at their briefings receive the unpleasant news that the weather is "extremely bad and that cumulonimbus clouds (thunderheads) will cover the route to the target up to 20,000 feet." Above four miles the night will be clear; this last bit of information is worthless for the bombers on the way to Hamburg, as their machines cannot hope to reach 20,000 feet, let alone fly through the thinner air above.

It is this forecast of violent weather conditions that gives Hamburg its first succor in this final drama of *Gomorrah*. Originally an all-out attack was to bring to its thundering close the Battle of Hamburg, and the bomber force would include all three of the British heavyweights—Stirlings, Halifaxes, and Lancasters. But there is the knowledge that the Halifaxes and Stirlings, most especially the latter, will be unable to climb above the peak of the clouds, and that to chance a long-range mission in these heavily-loaded machines will be to court disaster. Not only will the weather include severe turbulence, thick clouds, and rain, but icing conditions prevail in the skies along the route to be flown. This could easily mean that the lesser-performing bombers would be forced to jettison their bomb loads and, even then, would be inviting disaster because of severe ice.

Lancaster

Only the Lancaster has the strength and the performance to lift its tons of bombs above the clouds, and the monarch of the night bombers assumes alone the burden of Act Four of *Gomorrah*. What this raid is like—from the standpoint only of reaching the target—is best illustrated by the experience of Flight Lieutenant Robert Burr of No. 44 (Rhodesia) Squadron.

At Burr's field, the Lancasters taxi to the active runway in a seething downpour. The clouds hang low over England, and the sky seems almost to be drowning from the teeming mass of rain. Yet there is no recall; the bombers will go out. One by one the great machines trundle to the starting point of the runway, wheels sending water splashing heavily. Burr locks his brakes, runs the motors up, and quickly gives the Lancaster its freedom. It accelerates through the pounding rain like a dinosaur plunging through a swamp, trumpeting its power in an avalanche of sound, hurling up an enormous spray in its accelerating passage. Water streams from the wheels, hammers at the underside of the fuselage, whips into froth as it is spat away from the whirling propellers. Faster and faster, until there is only the hammering of water against the metal skin, and the crash of rain against the windscreen that drowns out all visibility in the cockpit.

The wings clutch the air and drag the bomber into the blackness. Wheels up at once; Burr eases back the control column and almost immediately the thick base of a huge thunderhead swallows up the climbing airplane and hurls a blinding fury of turbulent wind and rain at the machine. Burr brings up the flaps, and then his every second is spent in struggling simply to remain airborne, for he is in the midst of incredible violence, of vertical wind currents exceeding a hundred miles per hour. Lightning smashes open the blackness, great forked tongues of raging energy that disappear in an instant, leaving only the startling image on pained retinas. Burr stares at nothing but his instruments; they are his only contact with the normal world.

The airspeed indicator has gone crazy; it fluctuates by forty and fifty miles per hour, the needle flickering back and forth so rapidly that it is impossible to get an accurate reading. The rate-of-climb indicator, too, wobbles crazily, up and down. One moment it shows the heavy Lancaster climbing at two thousand feet a minute; the next second, the needle snaps down, and if it is reading correctly the bomber is dropping earthward at three thousand feet a minute.

In the cockpit Burr hangs grimly to his controls, fighting his ponderous machine every foot, every second. The rest of the crew hang on desperately, clutching anything that will prevent them from being buffeted about and whacked solidly against the frame-work of the aircraft. The Lancaster is helpless as a rowboat in a wild sea. The air buffets and slams against the machine as if to tear loose the wings and dash the invader of the storm to wreckage far below. Under the best of circumstances, to fly through such a storm is a forbidding experience; to do so in an airplane loaded to its maximum with bombs and ammunition and fuel is akin to suicide. And yet Burr's Lancaster is not alone in this violence of nature ...

The engines thunder, roaring defiance to the storm. Slowly but surely they lift the struggling bomber to greater heights, but it is a painful, heartbreaking ascent. Fifty hard won feet are lost in an instant as a powerful downdraft snatches at the bomber and drags it back to the level it has fought its way up from. And then, just as swiftly, a rising current of air slams the bomber from beneath and pushes it another fifty to a hundred feet higher.

Burr manages to fight the Lancaster in a laboring, grueling climb to 16,000 feet. At this altitude, still fighting every foot of his flight, the lieutenant sets his course over the North Sea, moving on a line that will take his Lancaster—as other pilots also will fly—toward the final massive blow at Hamburg.

There is no respite during this flight. Simply to keep the heavy bomber in level flight demands the constant and unremitting attention of its pilot. It is a nightmare of flying, a mission in which weather surmounts the dangers of the enemy, and becomes a foe much more deadly and effective.

At 17,000 feet the bomber refuses to climb any higher. It is no longer constantly within the furious storms; now it floats between giant mountains. Towering peaks loom far above, and beyond them are the stars. The Lancaster drifts through a world in which it is an insignificant mote, a tiny winged machine dwarfed by the immensity of lofty pinnacles, the weather ramparts of nature.

Then, without warning, nature reveals a hidden weapon, one that it has held in check, has refused to play in the stakes of life-or-death. From darkness lit by brief moments of the palest light oozes a strange lightning that clutches at the airplane. It is a lightning without thunder, no jagged streaks blaze through the sky. It is a personal, hellish fire, persistent, frightening, immediate.

The pilot: "All the metal parts of the aircraft shone with the blue spikes of St. Elmo's fire ... About a quarter mile to port was another aircraft flying on a parallel course. It seemed to be a mass of flames and I realized that it, too, must be covered with St. Elmo's fire. I stared at this flying beacon and ... suddenly, as I watched, a streak of lightning split the heavens. There was a huge flash and burning fragments broke away. The blazing wreckage tumbled into the clouds and disappeared ..."

Hamburg lies cloaked beneath its layer of clouds and the intermittent teeming rain. The bombers struggle to find their target areas, but the task is an impossible one. One hour after midnight the first bombs begin to fall. Mixed with the rain from the clouds is a cascade of 1,426 tons of high explosive

153

and incendiary bombs. Compared to the previous raids it is a poor effort, nevertheless, it is still a major blow. It is impossible to find any focal point in the raid, for the bombs scatter over the whole of the city. Many of them explode in the gutted firestorm areas with deafening roars that go unheard, for there are only the dead here, lying in the streets or entombed in the sealed shelters. The city is now emptied of more than a million of its people, and the bombs that crash into the undamaged areas often shatter buildings already abandoned by their normal tenants.

There is a temptation to pass off the effects of this final attack that rings down the curtain on *Gomorrah* as minor and relatively unimportant. But more than fourteen hundred tons of bombs are flung into the city, and on any scale this is a terrible blow. To the stunned and dazed survivors it has less impact only because their minds are hollow, their feelings rubbed to numbness. They do not know that the Bomber Command of the Royal Air Force has struck the city of Hamburg from its target list.

For the British, *Gomorrah* has reached its enormously successful conclusion. In the four major attacks, the last of which contributed little to the massive damage, Bomber Command dispatched a total of 3,095 heavy bombers. Of this number, 2,630 raiders reached and struck the target city. Into Hamburg there has poured a torrent of 8,261 tons of bombs, of which 4,309 tons were incendiaries.

Bomber Command has fought successfully the Battle of the Ruhr, and can now write off the Battle of Hamburg as finished business. The next battle, which Bomber Command is determined to wage with even fiercer onslaughts, will be the Battle of Berlin.

All this is unknown in Hamburg. The last bomb of *Gomorrah* has fallen, but for the city and its dazed inhabitants, the battle is far from over. There is still the aftermath of the great raids, and in certain respects this is worse even than the British enemy at the peak of his fury.

11

AFTERMATH

The story told thus far of the Battle of Hamburg is little more than a series of side dramas in the greater tragedy of the Hanseatic city. It is impossible to tell of the whole, for to the citizens of the shattered city it has been a wild struggle maintained without interruption for ten full days and nights, an endless river of terror punctuated with the blinding hours of actual attack, the ear-splitting roar of the exploding bombs and the firestorm howl that follows.

In the minds of the survivors the accumulated effects of attack and its staggering aftermath will never be forgotten. Flames and bombs by night and day displayed the aftermath of horror in the dim and unreal light of a sky suffocating in dense, almost impenetrable smoke. It is the height of the summer, intensified by the fierce heat radiating from the areas recently burned and still too hot to enter. The city swims under an oppressive blanket that is almost beyond human endurance. The air is fouled with soot and cinders and minute bits of floating debris.

Dust from the earth that has been torn and

gouged mixes with the smoke that rises from the still smoldering ruins. The choking atmosphere blocks out light, clogs the nose and stings the eyes, cakes in the pores and scratches throats to raw and red flesh. Soot and ashes swirl through the macabre metropolis; the slightest breeze brings up eddies of dust.

Above all there is the pestilential stench of decaying corpses, the sickening sweetish smell of roasted human flesh. It is a smell to drive men out of their minds, to chip away at the thin edge of their remaining sanity. The stench penetrates everywhere, and to keep it out men and women alike unconsciously restrict their respiration to shallow breathing. But they must breathe, and a careless deep breath brings on a spasm of nausea that sends a man to his knees, retching violently.

Thousands of individual fires still smolder; the smoke is heavy with the odor of death and burning corpses. Firemen and volunteers spend much of their time trying to save important buildings of the city; pitifully few have remained intact. This is a process of continual damping down of the smoking, smoldering areas, and it is a task they will perform for many weeks to come.

Days of terror and sickness and utter despair, of dejection so severe it drags down the soul. The survivors labor in the oppressive heat and the choking dust and the endless procession of death and destruction. There is no time for rest, there is no hope of salvaging anything in homes or apartments. There is nothing but the fierce struggle for life. Men and women who escaped the flames find they cannot even search for their children or other loved ones. All is flaming devastation and chaos compounded.

Hamburg ... degenerates. It is a city rotting and decaying, without gas or water or light. Most of the streets are impassable to traffic. Stony and ash-choked deserts are all that remain of once-flourishing residential districts.

For days afterward the streets of Hamburg are covered with corpses by the thousands. The bodies alone are savage testimony to the furious destruction the city has suffered. There are mothers with their children, youths, elderly men and women, and many of these are hardly recognizable as human creatures who walked and acted with dignity and purpose. They are burned and charred, and some are little more than ghostly shrivelled lumps. These are corpses untouched by any mark and fully clothed, people who were felled in an instant as they walked or ran, or stood petrified with fear. There are people who have died from sheer and overwhelming fright, who simply ceased to live.

Thousands of the bodies are naked, with a waxen pallor like dummies in a shop window. They lie in every posture, quiet and peaceful, or cramped in agony, with the struggle of death seared into their lifeless charred faces.

The shelters are nests of horror. Each day decontamination crews discover thousands more corpses to add to the soaring casualty lists. The city officials attempt to recover the dead according to their prepared plan, but it is a hopeless task. Many shelters that held hundreds of people are now buried beneath great mounds of debris, and removing these obstacles will take weeks. In many instances the debris is still so hot that the heat radiation prevents rescue and decontamination teams from even approaching the mass entombments.

Dozens of shelters are opened successfully, but the work crews are forced to run for their lives. The air trapped within the shelters is so hot that when the doors are opened the influx of oxygen causes the entire shelter to burst into flames! There are many shelters which have been opened or partially entered, and which must be left alone for ten days to two weeks in order that they may cool off sufficiently to allow any work.

In many of the shelters the number of dead can only be estimated. The sight is grisly beyond all imagination. The bodies have melted in with the general debris—these are the shelters in which glass, steel and other objects have melted, and the brick has become a soft and fine ash. There are hundreds of bodies added to the death lists from nothing more than the remains of a few bones.

Amidst these centers of absolute devastation, the decontamination teams uncover some shelters where the corpses are untouched by heat or flame. Their bodies are sitting quietly, as if sleeping in their chairs. Death has come without any warning or pain, as a result of carbon monoxide poisoning.

And there are shelters in which clear evidence is found of insane panic, of people who clawed at walls and flung their bodies headlong at stone barriers to escape when the heat became too great and pain stripped them of their reason.

Four months after *Gomorrah* came to its shattering climax, the Police President of Hamburg stated in his report that "Damping down had to be continued for a long time. Until August 25 this work had to be done daily and after that, in some places, until the beginning of October. Men of the motorized Air Protection battalions were employed to assist in Hamburg by day until August 7, and groups of the Armed Forces until August 10.

"...besides disposal of the dead one of the main duties of the Decontamination Columns was later the removal of phosphorus bombs and their residues. This work is not finished to this day. From August 26, fifty per cent of Fire and Decontamination personnel were employed in assisting the Rescue and Repair Service to clear the streets, removing tottering ruins with explosives and freeing buried cellars. This work will go on for months..."

There are other excerpts from the Official Report which are particularly germane to this book; told in the official language of the report they assume unusual significance:

"The heaviness of the raids was not without effect on the appropriate organization of the municipal authorities for the disposal of dead persons. This organization, however, would in any case have been unable to cope with such quantities of dead. For the carrying out of this work the Decontamination Sections, numerous auxiliary personnel of the armed forces, of the Technical Emergency Service and *de-*

160

tachments of prisoners from concentration camps were placed at the disposal of the Rescue and Repair Service. This utilization by the (Service) was only justifiable because the piled up heaps of hot debris caused by the enormous fires in the masses of brick did not permit of handling in the hitherto usual way. Where this was attempted work had often to be stopped so as to give time for cooling, in some cases for as long as ten days.

"...the Rescue and Repair Service was employed in cordoning off a so-called 'Dead Zone' and in all the work appertaining to it. The 'Dead Zone' embraced the adjoining districts in Rothenburgscort, Hammerbrook and South Hamm which were completely devastated, and from which most of the dead had to be recovered. The cordoning off of this 'Dead Zone' was carried out with materials quickly obtainable. Streets were shut off partly with barbed wire and to a considerable extent with dry masonry for which purpose the debris available was utilized. A few through roads were left open but closed off at the sides. The reason for the establishment of the 'Dead Zone' was the hitherto undreamed-of accumulation of corpses which at first gave rise to fears of disease. It was considered intolerable that the recovery of bodies should be carried out in public. By the creation of a 'Dead Zone' many individual cordons around houses in danger of collapse were avoided and numbers of personnel saved who would otherwise have been on police duty in connection with the cordon."

Here is more on the matter of disposing of the dead: "...rapid disposal of all bodies was a matter of great urgency as putrefaction set in quickly owing to the great heat, and epidemics were therefore to be expected. It transpired, however, that there was danger of putrefaction from the warm weather or heated walls and debris only with those bodies which were not already carbonized or burnt to ashes. (It was) essential to employ all means and all personnel as effectively as possible. The magnitude of the task may be inferred from the fact that even today (three months later) recovery of bodies is not completed ...

"The work of actual recovery, i.e., the removal and loading of the bodies, fell to the auxiliary personnel. So that the numerous squads and their auxiliary personnel should not become confused in their work on the large number of air raid shelters in various conditions and degrees of recovery, and overlap or do double work in moving large masses of debris, all air raid shelters from which the dead had already been recovered were marked on principle with a circular sign about the size of a plate with colored lettering. Where the walls were no longer standing this was done on a conspicuous heap of debris.

"The Decontamination Service had the task of undertaking urgently and extensively necessary disinfection of persons and property. Personnel employed had to be thoroughly disinfected before meals and at the end of their day's work.

"Constant and thorough disinfection of vehicles employed for removal was also necessary. For this purpose facilities for the disinfection of persons and property and the washing of vehicles were obtained next to a bathing establishment. Here were available soap and water, liquid disinfectant, chlorinated lime (in powder and paste form) as well as boxes with chlorinated lime paste for shoes and several C-hoses for washing vehicles. Until the requisite supplies of chlorinated lime, which exceeded all amounts in readiness, were obtained, Losantin also had to be used.

"It was also the duty of the Decontamination Service to sprinkle chlorinated lime over bodies lying in the streets or recovered from air raid shelters. Only when the stench of advanced decomposition was drowned by the smell of chlorinated lime, which pervaded whole districts, could the strong feeling of nausea prevalent at first among the recovery squads be overcome. Entry into air raid shelters from which bodies were being recovered was often only possible with a gas mask, in which the filter had been replaced by a pad soaked in rum or cognac.

"It was necessary also to scatter chlorinated lime on floors where highly serous corpses had lain. In many otherwise dry shelters much moisture from corpses had to be dealt with. This necessitated equipping the men employed with gumboots. All personnel had also to be supplied with rubber gloves to guard against post mortem virus.

"The mental and physical strain on the men employed was quite extraordinarily severe, especially in view of the indescribable condition of some of the bodies.

"These measures, particularly the extensive use of chlorinated lime, were intended to ward off any epidemics that might be threatening. The work could only be carried out by giving the men employed alcoholic drinks and tobacco...

"...for reasons of morale, to avoid undesirable mass transport of bodies through the city, it was decided to burn them at the spot where they had been found or in open spaces in the firestorm area. Another reason for this was that many bodies when recovered were already disintegrated from decomposition due to the heat. Some were charred, others burnt to ashes. In some instances only parts of bodies were found. When, after deliberation, it was established that no danger of epidemic was to be feared, the burial of all victims in a common grave in the cemeteries was resumed on grounds of respect for the dead. The common graves were dug at first with excavators in order to ensure that the speed of the work kept up with the removal of the bodies; *later they were dug by prisoners from concentration camps.*"

The concluding portions of this report, signed by Major General Kehrl of the S. S., who served also as the Police President of Hamburg, included these statements:

"It cannot be sufficiently emphasized that the great damage did not occur because of insufficient air protection measures but in spite of the best possible air protection measures. Under an alternating rain of high explosive and incendiary bombs, and with the failure of the municipal water supply, area fires and firestorms were bound to occur in closely built-up and densely-populated areas, as every dwelling house contains a mass of inflammable material which, under favorable conditions, can quickly be set on fire. Roofs, floors, wooden staircases, furniture, beds, carpets, curtains, etc., present fuel for the flames and target areas, which, by reason of the concentration of dwelling houses in large cities, are multiplied many times over. The exposing of this fuel to innumerable incendiaries was the cause of the lightning spread of the fires. The circumstance that the dense volume of high explosive bombs and land mines dropped laid open roofs and smashed windows, removed the natural resistance offered by the method of construction for succeeding incendiaries and greatly intensified the spread of fire.

"Forces were therefore let loose by the enemy raids against which the employment of human forces was bound to be hopeless. The actual opportunities of fire fighting were the most unfavorable imaginable.

"The most devastating effect both actually and psychologically, was caused by the failure of the water supply. The water available was insufficient or often blocked from the beginning by the effect of high explosive bombs and land mines, or on account of fires caused in lower floors by phosphorus and liquid incendiary bombs. All this means that gallant air protection personnel, prepared for any sacrifice, were bound to fail in the firestorm areas. This is confirmed by the activities of the Air Protection Police and their auxiliaries, who performed heroic individual service with complete disregard of danger, but were still unable, with the slender forces at their disposal, to prevent the calamity."

12

NOTES ON THE BATTLE OF HAMBURG

To obtain a complete perspective of the massive British assault against Hamburg in the bombing campaign known as *Gomorrah*, I have consulted the extensive records of the United States Strategic Bombing Survey, and spent many hours talking with American and British observers who studied Hamburg and other devastated German cities.

Regardless of the extent of the destruction visited upon Hamburg, the subjective view could not be other than one of absolute horror. The firestorm, the pain, the savage noise, the appalling casualties and the terribly grim and bleak aftermath with the particularly sensitive and painful task of removing the tens of thousands of dead—all these were experiences coalesced into a single nightmare of the most painful nature.

It is most significant, therefore, that the objective study of Hamburg, performed by skilled and trained personnel to whom widespread devastation and mass death were subjects of technical and clinical dissection, substantiates conclusively the gruesome events as reported by German officials and, to a far greater degree, the painful memories of the citizens of that city who survived the attacks.

The Over-All Report of the U.S. Strategic Bomb Survey states that: "Many German cities presented partial areas of vast devastation. Perhaps the outstanding example was Hamburg, where a series of attacks in July and August of 1943 destroyed 55 to 60 per cent of the city, did damage in an area of 30 square miles, completely burned out 12.5 square miles, wiped out 300,000 dwelling units, and made 750,000 people homeless. German estimates range from 60,000 to 100,000 persons killed, many of them in shelters where they were reached by carbon monoxide poisoning."

The Summary Report of the U.S.S.B.S. states: "No subsequent city raid shook Germany as did that on Hamburg; documents show that German officials were thoroughly alarmed and there is some indication from interrogation of high officials that Hitler himself thought that further attacks of similar weight might force Germany out of the war."

The Strategic Bombing Survey personnel studied the effects of firestorms which were raised by massive incendiary–high explosive attack within 15 to 30 minutes of the first bomb drop. One of the cities suffering a violent firestorm was Kassel, and the studies of the events in this town provided the first proof that under the conditions of a firestorm as many as 70 per cent of all the victims could be brought to the state of death by carbon monoxide poisoning. This was the figure given for Kassel, with the remaining casualties divided evenly between death due to the effects of the blast of high-explosive bombs, and deaths arising from direct burns and the inhalation of hot gasses.

The Survey established clearly that the incidence of loss of life is a variable that can be connected as much to the total bulk of combustible buildings in the neighborhood as to any other factor. The Hamburg dense-fire areas, which have been described, often had buildings 75 feet in height on both sides of a street that was no more than 60 feet wide. These streets, as we have seen, became literally great fire-locks or flues down which sheets of flame poured to consume all human beings caught in the flues. In effect, the burning streets, fanned on by the bellows of the wind sucked into the center of the firestorm, became roaring blast-furnaces.

Because of its strictly objective and clinical nature, the special report, *The Effect of Bombing on Health and Medical Care in Germany*, released in December of 1945 by the U.S. Strategic Bombing Survey, is of especial interest, particularly the chapter titled "The Nature of Air Raid Casualties." Prepared by Captain Franz K. Bauer, Medical Corps, Army of the United States, it is concerned particularly with accounts of death in mass fires. Following are excerpts from this Report:

...a meeting was called by the inspector of sanitary and medical matters of the Luftwaffe to discuss the effects of the great incendiary raids on Hamburg in July and August of 1943. The meeting took place in Jueterbog in December, 1943, and was attended by

169

pathologists, medicolegal experts, pharmacologists, and physiologists, all of whom had extensive experience with this problem. They concluded that the most prominent causes of death studied at the time were:

(1) Causes of death from external injury:
   (a) Burial under rubble and debris and injury from flying fragments.
   (b) Secondary injuries through explosions (drowning, scalding, chemical burns, poisoning from by-products of exploded bombs).
   (c) Burns.
   (d) Tetanus secondary to burns where no serum was given prophylactically.

(2) Causes of death from internal injury:
   (a) Carbon monoxide poisoning in air raid shelters and occurring during rescue work.
   (b) Effect of heat through conduction and radiation in the presence of very high temperatures.
   (c) Overheating over a prolonged period of time through temperatures which, normally, can be tolerated for short periods only.
   (d) Dust inhalation; blocking of the upper respiratory passages and inhalation, with damage of the small bronchi and alveoli.
   (e) Carbon monoxide poisoning from bursting gas mains.
   (f) Sudden heart death through fright and exhaustion in cardiac patients.

(g) Blast injuries in which external injuries may be absent or which may be masked by external injuries.

...After studies and reports from other German cities became available it was evident that mechanical causes of death headed the list, as had been expected. Direct hits by bombs and the action of bomb fragments, burial under rubble, and burns, all associated with shock, were the main causes of death of air raid victims throughout Germany.

Injuries due to mechanical causes, fractures, dislocations, sprains, and contusions, were listed as typical of air raids. This proves that there is little reason to believe that air raid injuries to civilians are any different from those encountered in ordinary war medicine.

Shock must have played a tremendous role. Statistics from one hospital gave shock as a cause of death in 12.6 per cent of all patients hospitalized from bombed areas. (Italics mine: MC.)

HEAT

An incendiary attack, through the effects of heat (and carbon monoxide) would cause more dead than wounded, whereas in high-explosive raids mechanical injuries would outnumber deaths. The crowded conditions of a city, the height of apartment houses, the age of dwellings—all these are contributory factors toward the spread of fire and the outbreak of a panic. There is a difference between peacetime fires and fires subsequent to air raids, but the difference is only quantitative. Thus 16,000 buildings were aflame at the same time in Hamburg in July, 1943.

The effects of heat were classified as:

(1) The effect of direct heat of short duration through conduction or radiation, with production of burns proper.

(2) The effect of high temperatures over long periods of time which did not immediately lead to protein coagulation, but which caused a syndrome identical with that of heat stroke.

The time at which injury from heat occurs varies with several factors, such as the humidity of the air, the cessation of sweat production, and the amount of heat to which the body has been exposed. In humid air, heat stroke may occur at a temperature of 60°C. (140°F.) and does not need to be associated with subjective complaints. This accounts for the many bodies which were found dead in rooms from which escape would have been possible, and which were in a position not suggestive of agony before death occurred.

Police engineers in Hamburg estimated that temperatures in the burning city blocks were as high as 800°C. (1,472°F.). Literally hundreds of people were seen leaving shelters after the heat became intense. They ran across the street and were seen to collapse very slowly like people who were thoroughly exhausted. They could not get up. Many thus killed were found to be naked. Two explanations have been offered for this phenomenon; that flames spurted across the street with the speed of a tornado, and consumed the victims' clothing, singeing their skin, or that the intense heat made the clothes dissolve without actual fire. The shoes were usually the only covering left on the bodies.

Most of these people were not burnt to ashes when recovered, but dry and shrunken, resembling mummies. In many the intense heat had caused the skin to burst and retract over typical areas such as the elbow, the knee, the scalp, and the orbit. Baniecki thought that the cause of death in these cases was shock. In approximately 80 autopsies he found all organs shrunken, showing venous stasis with increased permeability of the small blood vessels. Damage to the chromatin in practically all cells of the abdominal organs and the lungs was also seen which this investigator attributed to the inhalation of superheated air. However, it has not been admitted that inhalation of superheated air was the actual cause of death.

RADIANT HEAT

Professor Rose, chief consultant in hygiene to the Air Ministry, summarized the effects of heat. Besides immediate contact with flames, he wrote, the effects of heat through hot air as well as radiation of hot gases and from objects is of great importance. The main factor seems to be radiation. It is primarily the poorly clothed skin which is affected, whereby it and the subcutaneous tissues are damaged. This accounts for the severe heat changes in women who do not wear more than stockings on their legs or not even stockings. In many cases, when stockings were worn, they were not even singed, although the skin and underlying structures were severely damaged. Radiation heat of over 225°C. (439°F.) can inflame clothes and air. Besides this local effect of heat, overburdening of the heat-regulating mechanisms of the body is important. This is brought about by a hindrance of the heat exchange between the body and the atmosphere. Thus many air raid shelters which had been closed off by rubble produced an atmosphere intolerable to the occupants. Heat damage was seen in members of rescue squads who entered basements and air raid shelters where proper ventilation had not been available for some time, but the disturbances encountered were insignificant. Some of these rescue workers complained of vertigo, drowsiness, and headaches which lasted a day or so.

During escape from overheated shelters through burning city blocks, the danger was chiefly from radiated heat. The inhalation of hot air can cause severe damage to the respiratory passages such as ulcerous necroses of the mucous membranes. Whether this is a separate entity or the changes are a part of the whole picture which lead to death is as yet unsolved. It should be kept in mind that the inhalation of dangerous gases or by-products of fires must be considered.

The actual street temperatures in large-scale fires could only be estimated. The degree of temperatures produced in incendiary raids gave rise to a question from the office of Professor Karl Brandt, commissar for sanitary and health matters for Germany. Professor Schuetz, a physiologist of Muenster, answered from the Institute of Aviation Medicine: The question concerned the effect on the human body of over-heating to 41°C. (106°F.) for eight hours. The answer is: in the tissues increased temperature up to 50°C. is followed by death of all cells, with subsequent vacuolization; higher temperatures are followed by shrinking and falling apart of the cells. According to Ludwig Aschoff, human cells die at 50°C., vescicles form in the tissues at 51°C. and hemolysis occurs at 60°C. Ganglionic cells are destroyed at 43°C. Animals die exposed to temperatures of from 60° to 100°C. in overheated rooms, usually in convulsions, after a few minutes to half an hour.

ATTACK ON HAMBURG, JULY 27–28, 1943

Professor Graeff, consulting pathologist to the *Wehrkreis X* (military defense area) in Hamburg, gave a very vivid description of the air raids on the night of July 27–28, 1943. The crowded conditions in a city of the size of Hamburg, with its few parks and large squares, the height of the apartment houses, and the age of the dwellings are all contributory factors to the magnitude of the catastrophe. Soon after the sirens had sounded—a little before midnight on a clear night—the first bombs dropped. The warning was adequate for everyone to go to his shelter or bunker, and thereby evacuate the streets. High explosives and "air mines" destroyed houses, creating craters in streets and courtyards, ruining lighting and the power supply not only in the city at large, but also in the individual blocks, and opening the gas and water mains (no gas escaped from the gas mains).

In several bomb craters water accumulated from the burst water mains ran into shelters and basements and thereby caused a great nuisance. At the same time incendiary bombs started fires which spread particularly in thickly inhabited parts of town in a very short period of time. Thus in several minutes whole blocks were on fire and streets made impassable by flames. The heat increased rapidly and produced a wind which soon was of the power and strength of a typhoon. This typhoon first moved into the direction of the fires, later spreading in all directions. In the public squares and parks it broke trees, and burning branches shot through the air. Trees of all sizes were uprooted. The "firestorm" broke down doors of houses and later the flames crept into the doorways and corridors. The "firestorm" *looked like a blizzard of red snowflakes*. (Italics mine: MC.) More scientifically, firestorm is a mass of fresh air which breaks into burning areas to replace the superheated rising air.

The heat turned whole city blocks into a flaming hell. Those who were still in the streets or for some reason had to leave their homes crowded into a high bunker (a concrete tower shelter) or into a subterranean air raid shelter. Thus the number of people in shelters was doubled and tripled over the number considered safe.

The first serious danger in houses which had not been hit and had withstood explosions nearby became apparent when the lights went out, the water stopped running, and cracks formed in the walls. Air raid wardens on the roofs were threatened by the "firestorm" and crumbling roofs. In many cases, windows and exits from shelters were blocked by rubble and thus the shelters were safe against fire. As the temperatures increased in the streets from the spread of large-scale fires many of the occupants of the air raid shelters realized the precariousness of the situation, yet very few tried to escape into areas not endangered by fire. In the course of hours the air in the shelters became increasingly worse. Matches or candles did not burn. People lay on the floors because the air was better there and they could breathe easier. Some vomited and became incoherent. Some became tired and quiet and went to sleep. In some shelters oxygen cylinders were available and produced better breathing conditions for at least a short period of time. Wherever the ventilators were still working they brought in hot smoky air instead of cool fresh air, so that they had to be turned off. Filters, when available, proved insufficient to keep out smoke. The apparent safety of many shelters and basements closed in by rubble was only temporary as the approaching fire increased heat and smoke. In others, detonations and explosions nearby increased the pressure downward and directed the storm against the basements.

Thus the picture changed from hour to hour. Whoever was still able to make his own decision had one of two alternatives: to stay or escape. Many looked into the streets, saw that everything was on fire, decided they could not get through, and withdrew into the corners of the shelters. Some tried to get out of the burning areas and for them it was a race with death among explosions, fire bombs, machine guns, and falling flak. Besides all this, flames spurted through the streets and the wind caught up with many and threw them to the ground. There were screams from victims all around. No eyewitness mentioned screams with pain. Many people were caught in the fire. Many stated that the air "just didn't come any more" and breathing became very difficult. Otherwise they did not feel anything, and the rest went on over those who had fallen. One man was observed to fall. He was about to pull himself up with his hands when the flames were seen to envelop his back and he burned within five minutes without changing his position.

The dead usually lay with their faces toward the ground. Many were lying in rows. Only a very few who had fallen got up by their own effort or with the help of others and reached safety in the areas which had not been hit. Some found safety in the bottom of a bomb crater; others found death by drowning in other water-filled craters.

Every possibility of escaping the "firestorm" behind rubble or remaining walls or corners was kept in mind. This was evident by the number of corpses found behind these ledges and corners. The same was true in open spaces where many sought safety behind tree stumps and parked cars.

The only safe refuge in all this time was the water of the canals and the port. Most of those who got there were entirely exhausted. Lips, mouth and throat were dry. They were blistered on the nose and ears, on the hands and face, and their eyes burned with pain and could hardly be opened after having been exposed to so much smoke. Many collapsed, then lost consciousness and died. Many jumped into the water. Even here the heat was hardly bearable. They took blankets and handkerchiefs, soaked them in the water, and then protected their heads and the uncovered parts of their bodies with the wet cloths. But the water evaporated so quickly that this procedure had to be repeated every few minutes.

It is striking that thirst was not a generalized symptom. Some victims could not take enough water, yet some in utmost danger of heat death denied a feeling of thirst. They did not seek water, although water was available, nor did they report that they sweated more than normally. Others, however, took off their sweat-soaked clothes as soon as they had reached areas safe from fire and excessive heat.

Only a few generalizations could be made from the remarks of those who came to safety. In the first hours after they had successfully escaped, some complained of headaches and slight drowsiness. The desire for sleep was present in all and sleep very deep. After awakening there were no sequelae.

THE HELL THAT WAS LEFT BEHIND

In the meantime the burned-out houses caved in. The rubble and debris on the streets prevented many from escaping. The heat decreased slowly, but the main danger was past. Many of the bodies were lying in the streets half clothed or nude.

The only covering that they always had on were

their shoes. The victims' hair was often burned, but frequently preserved. A few hours after the start of the raid the corpses had a peculiar aspect; they seemed blown up, lying on their stomachs. The buttocks were enlarged and the male sex organs were swollen to the size of a child's head. Occasionally the skin was broken and indurated in many places and in the majority of cases was of a waxen color. The face was pale. This picture lasted only a few hours; after this time the bodies shrank to small objects, with hard brownish black skin and charring of different parts and frequently to ashes and *complete disappearance*. [Emphasis added.]

At the same time fate had caught up with many of those in the shelters and the basements. In houses which had caved in through the effect of high explosives or fires, the bodies were found covered with rubble. The air raid tower shelters and also the larger number of the subterranean shelters withstood the explosions and fire. There was no doubt that in many a shelter, death had come to the occupants without anyone ever suspecting it. Several persons were sometimes found sitting or lying in the most natural position; others were sitting in groups as if talking to each other and some had slipped to the floor from chairs or benches. The absence of defense or escape movements could not be explained other than as death without premonition. In many shelters, however, bodies were found in a heap in front of the exit so that it must be concluded that escape was sometimes attempted.

In the shelters bodies assumed various aspects

corresponding to the circumstances under which death had set in. Nowhere were bodies found naked or without clothing as they were in the streets. The clothes, however, often showed burned-out holes which exposed the skin. Bodies were frequently found lying in a thick, greasy black mass, which was without a doubt melted fat tissue. The fat coagulated on the floors as the temperature decreased. The head hair as a rule was unchanged or only slightly singed. The bodies were not bloated except for a few which were found floating in water which had seeped into the shelters from broken mains. All were shrunken so that the clothes appeared to be too large. Those bodies were called "incendiary-bomb-shrunken bodies"—*Bombenbrandschrumpfleichen.* They were not always in one piece. Sleeves and trouser legs were frequently burned off and with them the limbs were burned to the bones. Frequently such bodies burned to a crisp weeks after death—apparently after oxygen had become available. In the same rooms with such bodies were found other more or less preserved or shrunken corpses and also some which had fallen to ashes and could hardly be recognized. Many basements contained only bits of ashes and in these cases the number of casualties could only be estimated.

Carbon monoxide as a major cause of death after aerial bombing was a possibility which few had expected before the war. It is now recognized as a typical "shelter or cellar death." Like heat it occurred in rooms the exits of which were blocked by rubble or fire. In such cases, the origin of the carbon monoxide was always incomplete combustion. Also, in many instances, as much as 70 per cent of the gases liberated from an exploded bomb was carbon monoxide.

Carbon monoxide death assumed such importance that the high command of the Luftwaffe issued an order to examining commissions to procure statistical evidence of carbon monoxide poisoning. In death resulting from burial in rubble, carbon monoxide poisoning was often the real cause of death. This is not surprising when it is kept in mind that many fires start when a house caves in, in bombing by incendiaries as well as by high explosives.

Death attributable to carbon monoxide was also known to occur in the open. The additional strain of an attempt to escape from fire and heat was often the difference between life and death. That carbon monoxide will damage an already diseased heart muscle more than a normal one, is well known. That carbon monoxide is taken up in increased quantities when respiration is rapid is obvious. In a fire developed after a raid on Wesermeunde, of 210 corpses, 175 presented the picture of acute carbon monoxide poisoning. In Hamburg, 70 per cent of all casualties apart from those resulting from mechanical causes or burns were caused by monoxide. According to one observer a concentration of 0.5 per cent carbon monoxide in the air can cause death after one hour. Even a concentration of 0.1 per cent may still produce symptoms. This observer also states that the old theory that one cannot die in a room where a flame can still burn is incorrect. The reason is that, as has been mentioned, the concentration of 4 per cent coal or lighting gas (corresponding to 0.5 per cent carbon monoxide) will lead to death after one hour, whereas explosion does not occur until a concentration of between 8 and 16 per cent is attained. Fumes from ordinary fires are said to contain 3 per cent of carbon monoxide gas, coal gas to contain 6 per cent carbon monoxide, gas from a high-explosive bomb 60 per cent to 70 per cent carbon monoxide.

Qualitative and quantitative examinations for carbon monoxide were carried out in Hamburg and several other cities throughout Germany. A reliable laboratory test (Ponsold) was reported to be: One drop of blood from a corpse is added to 50 cc. of water. If this retains its red color, carbon monoxide hemoglobin is present. If not, the test should be regarded as negative for carbon monoxide. High temperatures will destroy carbon monoxide hemoglobin. Putrefaction will not destroy carbon monoxide hemoglobin. The conclusion as to the importance of carbon monoxide poisoning as a cause of death in incendiary raids on large German cities is plainly dependent on the validity of this statement concerning the presence of carbon monoxide in the blood at a considerable time after death.

The conclusion arrived at by the German authorities was that there was a need for a good and sensitive test for the detection of carbon monoxide in living and dead persons, because in the hands of most investigators the tests were unreliable in people who had been dead more than a few hours.

Concentrations up to 95 per cent were found in many "shelter dead." The fact that many shelters and basements could not be entered for many days after a raid made qualitative and quantitative examinations for carbon monoxide unreliable or even impossible. The typical characteristic of carbon monoxide deaths in aerial war is the so-called peaceful position of the bodies, which is suggestive of complete lack of apprehension of danger.

13

NOT IN THE RECORDS

There is one episode in the ten-day bombing of Hamburg that stands out sharply as perhaps the single most grisly incident of all the aerial attacks of World War II. I have spent several years in an attempt to track down as many specific details of this matter as could be obtained, and have met with less than the success required by the historian to include the episode in a documentary book. My research contacts have included survivors of Hamburg who swear to the authenticity of this story; I have discussed the matter also with Allied observers who participated in the studies of the effects of our bombing attacks on Germany. From all these sources, and from "leads" that persistently cropped up in survivor reports, I have assembled every last scrap of information. Perhaps the solution to the total absence of any reference in official German documents is explained in the story told to me by a U.S. Army officer, who learned that portions of the documents on the after-effects of the Hamburg attacks were ordered to be destroyed, and all references to the surviving victims of phosphorus bombs stricken forever from the records.

In the Battle of Hamburg, the British bombs included the 30-pound missile of which the incendiary contents were phosphorus. The U.S. Strategic Bombing Survey reports officially that the "psychologic effect of phosphorus bombs was far greater than any actual damage which they caused." The report states that "phosphorus burns were not infrequent," but that most such burns "occurred in people who had come in contact with unexploded phosphorus canisters lying about in the streets and under the rubble . . ."

The U.S.S.B.S. report states further that "The direct contact with an exploding incendiary bomb is a freak, and was never seen in Germany."

I have specifically cited these statements in this chapter because I do not wish to leave out *any* material that is available on this matter of phosphorus bombs in the Hamburg attacks.

For what can be obtained *outside* of the records indicates that several hundred people out of a larger group *were* subjected to a spray of phosphorus material, with terrifying consequences. British reports of phosphorus bombs dropped by the Germans against English cities indicate that the use of this incendiary material was severe enough in its effects to drive the fire-fighting teams crazy. Whenever it dried out it immediately exploded into flames. You could cover phosphorus with sand and douse it with water, and it would stay quiescent. But the moment its covering— that restricted the air from the phosphorus—was gone, the flames immediately burst out again.

The British employed phosphorus because of its demonstrated ability to depress the morale of the

Germans. It is one thing to fight an incendiary bomb, and quite another when you face a bomb that persists in flaring into life again and again. Phosphorus sticks grimly to any surface it touches—metal, wood, concrete, clothing, or human flesh. Whatever the material, the phosphorus will cling to it for good (unless it is scraped off) and will continue to burn itself out unless it is permanently denied access to oxygen.

The incident in Hamburg we are concerned with involves the several hundred people on whom particles of phosphorus splattered in a great shower. It was at the height of the bombing; the great fires already were raging, and thousands of people were struggling frantically to escape the flames. Among these thousands were the several hundred who were caught directly in a dense shower of the phosphorus bombs.

The injury to those poor souls struck by the phosphorus was immediate. Wherever the incendiary material landed it immediately burst into flame. Clothing caught fire quickly and had to be ripped free of the body, or the wearer would suffer serious burns. When the phosphorus fell against a person's hair, that individual was doomed. There was no chance to cut off the hair, and the chemical globs blazed fiercely, setting aflame the entire head and burning against the skin itself.

These terrified and pain-wracked human beings were seen to leap about in a frenzy, or to dash their heads against the ground in a blind panic—anything to douse the flames. Immediately covering the burning hair with clothing—which will smother an ordinary fire—was useless with the phosphorus, which, being reached by some air, simply continued to burn and set afire the material thrown over it.

These things happened during the height of the panicky flight from the flames, and those who fell by the wayside, writhing in agony as the flames burned down into their skulls, were simply left to their fate.

A large number of the phosphorus victims were near the banks of the Alster. By the dozens these shrieking, hapless souls, trailing tongues of flame and smoke, dashed madly to the water to fling themselves headlong into the lifesaving liquid. Men and women and children, running hysterically, falling and stumbling, getting up, tripping and falling again, rolling over and over. The majority managed to regain their feet and the safety of the water. But not all—the others were left behind, feet drumming in blinding pain on the heated pavements and rubble, until there came a last convulsive shudder through the smoking thing on the ground, and then no further movement.

Those in the water found the safety they had sought so desperately—unless the phosphorus was on their heads or faces or necks. Water douses phosphorus by denying it the oxygen it needs to sustain combustion, and those with the flaming chemical on their arms and legs and bodies were able to extinguish the flames instantly on entering the water.

But those agonized souls who had the phosphorus on their faces and heads! Certainly the flames went out as they plunged into the water of the Alster. The moment they came up, however, the phosphorus received its oxygen and again burst into flames. And so began the unbelievable terror of choice—death by drowning or by burning.

If there were chemicals that could safely remove the phosphorus, those chemicals were not available during the height of the firestorm (the Alster lay at the periphery of the great mass blaze) in the heart of the city. A knife could scrape both the top layers of skin and the phosphorus from the body together, but who had presence of mind, a place to work, and the tools during *these* moments? Who, indeed, could even think with some trace of coherency? Remember that this was in the midst of the greatest mass fire the world had ever known, and terror and pain were rampant.

So while the others watched, sick and despairing, these victims of phosphorus on faces and heads thrashed wildly in the water, screamed in their pain and the madness of their utter frustration. Choking and spluttering, alternately burning alive and drowning, they met a slow and pain-wracked death. The wild motions ceased, the froth on the water slowly subsided. There were left the victims who had the phosphorus on their limbs and bodies; they were safe only as long as their burns were covered by water.

The great fire thundered to its climax; the orgiastic rampage of flame subsided. The victims who had survived the long night of blinding heat were a sorrowful huddle in the morning. They were on the edge of the infamous "dead zone" where heat radiation was so severe that no one could enter, and survive.

Those in the water who had not suffered phosphorus burns made their way as best they could to safety across the Alster. The others had no choice but to remain where they were, numb, in shock, physically and mentally exhausted. Their skin was blistered and suffering from the long exposure to the water.

There are few authentic reports available to us today to indicate what happened in those several days of ultimate human suffering. From what has been gleaned from all sources, the victims still in the water could not be removed. Hamburg was virtually a battleground, and there were neither the time nor the facilities for proper medical attention. Despite their agony, the sufferers in the water fought their would-be rescuers violently, for they knew the torture that would begin the moment they emerged from the water.

To the limit of their ability, the people who could—who would—come to their aid, attempted to ease the hellish torture of the phosphorus victims in the water. They brought them drinking water to sip, tried to attend to their visible wounds and burns. But there was no help, really, that could be provided. The people in the water were the living dead.

Their skin began to slough off. Their burns festered and thick pus oozed out. Blisters broke to expose raw meat beneath, and the suffering humans became little more than animals in agony moaning through blistered and bleeding lips. It went on like this, hour after hour, until darkness fell once more. And from the blackened surface of the water these once-human creatures cried out from the depths of their agony.

They could no longer remain awake, and they struggled to brace themselves against bollards and posts while their hapless benefactors helped support them as best they could. As the burns and the wounds began to exert their full effect, and the continued exposure of the water slipped the skin from their bodies like a peeling snake, not a few went completely mad.

They were not human beings, and they were unlike any animal ever known on this earth. Insanity showed in their eyes, the tortured, gleaming eyes. Their teeth snapped together with grisly, skeletal clicking sounds. They shrieked and cried out and moaned; caught in a sucking whirlpool of ultimate horror they cursed their families and loved ones and their God, calling down damnation upon those who would leave them thus, to suffer endlessly.

Late that night—in the hours of the morning—the last civilians were removed by German officials and military personnel. The area was sealed off. Small boats bearing the police and the soldiers moved among the stumps of heads in the water, and along the shore. More than one man became sick and vomited that night.

Above the splash of oars against water, and the moaning, came the sound of a metallic click.

It was a distinct sound, the cold metallic warning of a Luger pistol's toggle breech snapping shut as the first round is chambered. And then ... a shot rang out. Another, and another, and another.

The boats moved quietly among the stumps. More shots, and more.

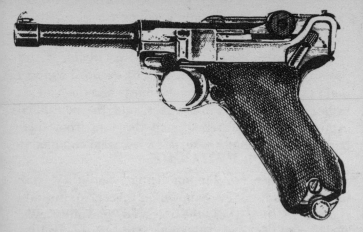

Luger P-08

Some of the boats ran out of ammunition. There were sharp thuds, the crack of heavy oars against human skulls.

It was the only mercy that could be administered. It was the only peace that could be found.

It was all over by the first sign of the dawn that struggled through the smoke pall hanging over the grave of Hamburg.

EPILOGUE

The Battle of Hamburg passed into history. In ten days the fiery bombardment had brought death to more than one hundred thousand human beings and produced destruction on a scale that might have appalled even Attila or Ghengis Khan.

Never before had there been a fire so vast, so destructive or all-consuming. Never before had so many people been trampled into lifelessness—and even obliterated entirely from existence—by the work of man. The Battle of Hamburg, which had given to *Gomorrah* a new and fiery meaning, became in its passing a mark of comparison with all mass fires before—and since.

Hamburg established new levels of death, horror, and destruction; for size and intensity of fire, not even the atomic bombings of Hiroshima and Nagasaki equaled the flaming devastation sown in the Hanseatic port. By the close of World War II only one city was known to have exceeded Hamburg in area destroyed in a single mass attack, and in numbers of people killed.

This was Tokyo. On the night of March 9–10,

B-29

1945, a swarm of giant B-29 bombers—great airplanes that dwarfed even the British Lancaster—put the torch to the heart of the Japanese capital. In a great sweep conflagration, a wall of flame moving before a high wind, the natural inflammability of the great Japanese city became its death warrant. Sixteen square miles of that city, teeming with people, vanished within a few hours. More than 136,000 human beings burned to death or died as a direct result of the mass wall of fire.

At Hiroshima, 80,000 people died in an area approximately the same size as the firestorm area gutted in Hamburg on the second major raid. At

Nagasaki, a much smaller area was obliterated, and some 35,000 people died.

Then, shortly after the end of the fighting, there were received from the Russian zone of occupation disturbing reports of a firestorm even greater in its death-toll than the one that had raged at Hamburg. The area involved was smaller, but the reported casualties were beyond belief. The city: Dresden. The time: the night of February 13–14, 1945. The British bombing force: *one* heavy attack in two waves.

By February of 1945, great armadas of heavy bombers thundered over German soil with what amounted to impunity from enemy defenses. Not only had the attacks of the Army Air Forces on a sweeping circle from the Scandinavian countries down through the Channel coastland, all the way into Italy and the Mediterranean, achieved an unbelievable tempo, but the heavy bombers of the Royal Air Force were even operating frequently in daylight. The battering of Germany reached a crescendo beyond all imagination. While the American raiders continued to isolate and hack to pieces the so-called precision targets (although a massive stream of Fortresses in a single daylight attack killed nearly 40,000 citizens of Berlin), the Royal Air Force continued its mission of piling ruin upon ruin in German cities, slaughtering tens of thousands of workers, injuring hundreds of thousands, burning vast sections into rubble, immobilizing millions of workers, and extinguishing the economic substance of the Reich. In effect, by the end of February the once-mighty Nazi Germany was no longer a nation of recognizable industrial might.

The war, however, was far from its end, and there was still violent and terrible fighting under way. Because of this continued struggle in the face of imminent defeat, the Germans brought upon themselves a torrent of flaming ruin. The obligations of the United States and England to the Russians included a maximum effort to shatter the German transport system that supported fighting on the Eastern Front. A key element of this system was the railway center of Dresden; the "German Florence," considered to be the loveliest rococo city in Europe, had become not only the main center of communications through which flowed German arms, but it was also the headquarters for the army groups fighting on the southern half of the Eastern Front.

The city, with a prewar population of 633,000, had never been bombed, and it is likely that had not the Germans put Dresden to such belated but vital use in its ground fighting, it might never have felt the shock wave of a single explosion. Be that as it may, it had leaped to prominence as a transportation center, and the Russians specifically requested of the Anglo-American bombing commands that Dresden be immediately "neutralized."

But Dresden no longer had its "normal prewar population of 633,000 people." Since the first week in January, millions of Germans had fled in terror from their homes in the Warthe District and in Silesia before the advancing tide of a vengeful Red Army that slaughtered, raped, burned, tortured and pillaged in a vendetta of fantastic proportion. The roads and trains, the villages and the towns of Saxony, the

Sudetic Mountains, and nearby areas were swollen with refugees.

It was a scene not unlike the early days of World War II, when refugee columns rushed in panic before another army that also heralded its advance with the same rape, murder and torture, mass hangings and executions that characterized the Soviet onslaught. In those days the army was German; now, by the judgment of war, the tables were turned. It was a retribution the news of which brought grim satisfaction to many millions.

And it was also an evacuation of incredible suffering, for the long processions and caravans of fleeing Germans moved through a bitter and fierce winter. They sought the safety of distance over ice-glazed roads and subzero temperatures; they struggled through snow, weary, footsore, and hungry. But there was no thought of ceasing the flight; the specter of the Red Army drove them onward.

Despite the best efforts of the German authorities to detour these long processions around the now-vital hub of Dresden, the human tide spilled into the city by the tens of thousands. The streets were black with people waiting for space aboard trains; they stood on the sidewalks of Dresden, in the streets, on the Elbe Meadows. On the night of February 13, 1945, the railway station in Dresden was jammed with refugee trains, and with uncounted thousands who stood shoulder to shoulder and fought for space.

A paradox of Dresden's critical position in the war at that time was its helplessness against air attack. The German night fighter force, thrown into the daylight air battles as a stop-gap measure to halt the American Fortresses and Liberators, had been slaughtered by the far-ranging Thunderbolts, Lightnings, and Mustangs escorting the bombers. By mid-February of 1945 they could offer only token resistance to the night raiders of the British. Since Dresden had never been bombed, and its guns were sorely needed elsewhere, Adolf Hitler stripped the city of all its antiaircraft guns and despatched them to the Oder.

Thus Dresden stood naked to air assault. How many people were in the city this night of February 13–14 will never be known accurately, but there seems to be no question that from 750,000 to a million refugees had added to the normal population. The first attack came at that moment when the trains were still in the city, and had not yet begun the evacuation of the desperate refugees.

A force of 244 Lancasters came over the city in a massed wave. For 26 minutes, from 10:09 to 10:35 P.M., they poured a concentration of high explosive and incendiary bombs into the very heart of the Saxony capital. The older quarters of the city, jammed with highly inflammable buildings, ignited with blinding speed, and within minutes a vast section of Dresden was a scene of roaring flames.

One of the pilots in the first wave reported that "The town looked very beautiful ringed with searchlights, and the fires in its heart were of different colors. Some were white, others of a pastel shade

Lockheed P-38

outlined with trickling orange flame. Whole streets were alight ... Yet, as I went over the target, it never struck me as horrible, because of its terrible beauty."

Then, at 22 minutes past one o'clock the morning of the 14th, the second wave struck, much more powerful than the first. This time the force included a total of 529 Lancasters, and they rushed in to a city with their targets clearly marked for them. There was little use in hurling their bombs into the already burning areas, so the Lancasters simply headed for the districts still free from fire, and concentrated their explosives and incendiaries in these sections. When the last bomber turned to return to England,

Dresden had received the appalling total of 2,659 tons of bombs and incendiaries, all within a limited area.

The second attack proved so fierce and concentrated that almost at once a screaming firestorm arose in the city. Because the built-up area was small, the storm encompassed a total of 1,600 acres. It was more than enough, for the population density was far greater than at Hamburg.

This factor alone accounted in great part for the staggering casualties that resulted. The great high-explosive bombs—up to 4,000 pounds in weight—poured a torrent of death and mutilation into the thick crowds still in the streets trying to escape from the fires set earlier into districts where safety beckoned.

By the paradox of war, one of the survivors of the bombing was an Englishwoman. Mrs. Riedl, married before the war to a German, had only that night reached Dresden as a refugee from Lodz in Poland. As the sirens sounded for the first raid, she rushed with several other women to a cellar for shelter. There were no street lights, but this mattered not at all, as the leaping flames from nearby building provided a harsh glare. Thirty minutes later, when the sirens sounded the all-clear signal, Mrs. Riedl rushed upstairs to plunge into a world in which "burning sparks were flying about like snowflakes."

By some miracle the house in which Mrs. Riedl had joined several women was not yet burning, although it seemed likely that this building too would soon be aflame. The women dashed through the rooms, tearing down curtains and rolling up carpets when the second alarm rang through the city.

Again they hurried to the shelter, but this time they did not remain for long. Thick smoke boiled into the small room and "we all began to choke."

Frantic, their exit blocked, the women kicked and knocked a series of holes through partition walls to reach the street. The scene facing them was grotesque, and they gasped in terror. Flames leaped and danced wildly in every direction, and the street, although fairly wide, had become a violent flue of wind and blazing sparks and firebrands.

Mrs. Riedl no sooner crawled through the hole from her shelter, when she took the blanket she had been carrying and thrust it into a tub of water that was nearby. Soaking the blanket until it was dripping wet, she flung it over her head and around her shoulders, and fought her way to the center of the street. Flight was impossible, for the surrounding streets, narrower and with higher buildings, were entirely swamped in flames.

The group of people crouched low in the center of their street for more than seven hours while the storm that raged nearby froze them in terror. Finally, there came the miracle of a brief but heavy cloudburst, temporarily damping the fires that surrounded them. At once they rose to their feet and fled, grateful for the temporary respite. This was the second move that saved their lives. By eight in the morning Mrs. Riedl and the others in her party were stumbling at the edge of the town, toward the river into which thousands of people had flung themselves.

The river banks, and the open spaces beside them, were unbelievable. The ground was choked with the bodies of thousands of human beings who were caught in the open by the furious weight of the second attack.

The Russians were forgotten for these terrible, flaming moments. The storm raged all through the night, and the bleak light of the smoke-suffocated dawn revealed streams of haggard, burned, and terrified refugees flowing into the open countryside and nearby towns, their eyes glazed and minds stunned beyond the edge of sanity.

That day even as the fires still raged, the people remaining in the city turned their eyes to the sky in stark disbelief. Three hundred and eleven Flying Fortresses of the Eighth Air Force poured an additional 771 tons of bombs into Dresden (other bombers attacked Chemnitz and Magdeburg), and added more thousands to the dead, and tens of thousands to the injured.

The bombing was done by radar, for it was impossible for the Fortress crews to see the city. A dense pall of black smoke hung over Dresden to a height of 15,000 feet. And the next day, February 15, 210 Fortresses came back in the finale, cascading 461 tons of bombs into the gutted wasteland that was Dresden. In the three raids, British and American forces had dropped nearly 4,000 tons of bombs.

The city was dead. Its industry was totally destroyed, its value as a communications center shattered completely. It no longer posed an operational problem for the Red Army.

It is appropriate here once again to quote the U.S. Strategic Bombing Survey:

"The city area raids have left their mark on the German people as well as on their cities. Far more than any other military action that preceded the occupation of Germany itself, these attacks left the German people with a solid lesson in the disadvantages of war. It was a terrible lesson; conceivably that lesson, both in Germany and abroad, could be the most lasting single effect of the air war."

The ruined and gutted cities of Germany offered mute but thoroughly effective testimony to that belief. More than a half million German civilians died in the attacks, nearly a million more suffered serious injury. Some twenty-five million Germans had known the terrifying sound and sight of the great air attacks.

The destruction of Hamburg culminated in an orgy of fire the world had never known before, and it brought about the immediate death of more than one hundred thousand human beings.

Consider the hideous ruin, then, of Dresden. Not merely the savagely burned out areas. Ignore the physical devastation, the obliteration of vast tracts of a beautiful city.

Consider only the dead.

More than three hundred thousand men, women, and children perished.

Truly Germany had sown the wind.

ABOUT THE AUTHOR

The author of over fifty books and more than a thousand magazine articles, MARTIN CAIDIN is one of the outstanding aeronautics and aviation authorities in the world. The National War College, the Air Force's Air University, and several other institutions use his books as doctrine and strategy guides, historical references, and textbooks. He has twice won the Aviation/Space Writers Association award as the outstanding author in the field of aviation: in 1958 for his *Air Force: A Pictorial History of American Airpower*, and in 1961 for *Thunderbirds!*

Mr. Caidin flies his own plane throughout the United States. He has also flown private planes to various countries, and bombers to Europe. He is rated for both landplanes and seaplanes, single-engine and multi-engine. For six weeks in 1960 he flew aerobatics in an F-100F Super Sabre with the famed Air Force Thunderbirds. He has also ridden in centrifuges, dived vertically at 1,100 mph, undergone explosive decompression in an altitude chamber, witnessed the firing of literally hundreds of missiles, rockets, and space vehicles, and toured military, research, and industrial installations throughout the United States.

Join the Allies on the Road to Victory
BANTAM WAR BOOKS

William L. Shirer

A Memoir of a Life and the Times Vol. 1 & 2

☐ 34204   TWENTIETH CENTURY JOURNEY,
               The Start 1904-1930 $12.95

☐ 34179   THE NIGHTMARE YEARS,
               1930-1940 $14.95

In Volume 1, Shirer recounts American/European history as seen through his eyes. In Volume 2, he provides an intensely personal vision of the crucible out of which the Nazi monster appeared.

Charles B. MacDonald

☐ 34226   A TIME FOR TRUMPETS $12.95
The untold story of the Battle of the Bulge.

THE STORY OF AN AMERICAN HERO